LETTERS FROM THE TRAIL
Blueberry*

*a.k.a. Peggy Alden Stout

Short—and Long-Distance Hiker on the Appalachian Trail
2000-2010

Graphite Drawings by Rainy Brooks

LETTERS FROM THE TRAIL

Excerpts from a collection of letters written by a
woman from Maine and Maryland as she pursued
a life goal of hiking the entire 2,150-plus-mile
Appalachian Trail after turning fifty.

Blueberry*

*a.k.a. Peggy Alden Stout

Short—and Long-Distance Hiker on the Appalachian Trail
2000-2010

Graphite Drawings by Rainy Brooks

To order additional copies of this book, contact:
Xlibris Corporation
1-888-795-4274
www.Xlibris.com
Orders@Xlibris.com
107729

CONTENTS

*I realized as I was organizing all these letters that I should probably divide them into topics or categories. The problem with that is the letters often focus on more than one topic! However, I'll give it a try and place them the best I can, based on what I've written. I have decided to use a question format as I think the letters can easily be adapted to answering the questions.

DEDICATED TO

- Marty, my husband, my love, and my main support and advocate, who was always there to help . . . and, without whom, I could never have done the hikes or put together this book.

- Jeff, my son, who has inspired me to follow my dreams.

- My father, Russell Alden, a Maine guide whose love and knowledge of the outdoors has always inspired me.

- My mother, Marion Philbrook Alden, who skied down Mt. Washington when she was twenty and who would have hiked the AT had she known about it in the 1930s.

Dear Reader,

I have been traveling parts of the Appalachian Trail since 1997 when I turned fifty. During each of my hikes, I have used letter writing to family and friends as a way of daily journaling about the trip. After each trip, the letters were sent back to me so I could keep a record of my thoughts, feelings, daily events, responses to questions about the trip, and all the other miscellaneous pieces of information I had gathered about long-distance hiking and the AT, in particular.

I have compiled the letters into this book, organizing them or parts of them around certain themes. I am using more recent letters to my niece Maria as the overall structure for the book and as a way to introduce various topics.

There is much to say about hiking the AT, and I hope the informality which these letters lend will allow you to feel a part of what I have experienced. There may be some letters which repeat information given in other letters; I have tried to use only parts of certain letters to eliminate that, but at times, I felt compelled to leave the whole letter intact because of the flow of information or thoughts.

As you read these letters, I hope that descriptions of the adventure of day-to-day life on the trail, the "community" of the AT, the satisfaction of being self-sufficient, and the unlimited time for self-reflection will convey the sense of why I am continually lured to hiking and the outdoors.

Enjoy!

The Appalachian Trail: a continuous 2,150-plus-mile footpath which spans the crest of the Appalachian Mountains from Mt. Katahdin in Maine to Springer Mountain in Georgia. The trail passes through fourteen states and some of the most scenic lands on the East Coast.

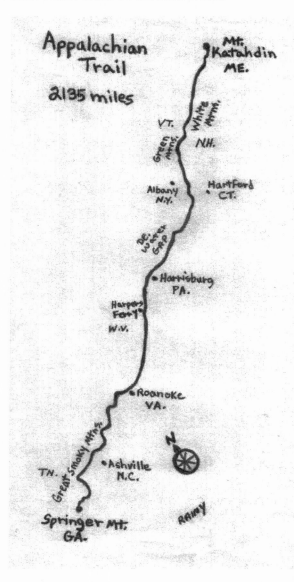

December 2008

Dear Maria,

It hardly seems like time for me to be writing to say congratulations on graduation from college! Just yesterday you were a little girl, and now it seems that you are on your way to being a full-fledged adult. I have such vivid memories of your early life and our first attempts to go camping . . . sleeping in our tent in the basement, sleeping part of the night in the tent at the edge of our lawn—and then just having you come for the campfires because you weren't sure that you liked camping! So what a surprise it was to us when you went away to college and we started hearing that you were going on camping trips to the Everglades and other places. Suddenly, you were loving camping, hiking, being outdoors, snakes, etc.! I was struck by your comment to me in March when

I'd been winter camping in Maine. You said, "Sometimes it's just good to get outside into the woods in the snow and cold." My sentiments exactly, and you were the only one who had responded to me that way about that trip.

I am delighted that you have discovered the power of the outdoors and are combining it with the power you have as a woman. You always have been one, even as a ten-year-old, who spoke your mind, who knew who you were and what you wanted to do. That is so important for a woman of the twenty-first century.

Like you, I have found over the years that I thrive on what the outdoors does for me. As you know, I have hiked the Appalachian Trail as a long-distance section hiker over the past ten years. I actually started traveling parts of the AT in 1997 when I turned fifty, beginning with day hikes in the Maryland section and, from there, moving into one—or two-week trips, as well as two two-month trips.

I have managed, at this point, to complete 2,000 miles of the 2,100-mile trail. Initially, most of my hiking was done alone which gave me an opportunity to know myself in a way that the normal life I lead does not. As you know, the beauty and solitude of the woods create a setting for self-reflection that is hard to replicate in any other setting.

I have to tell you that the overwhelming response when people heard that I was going to hike the AT was shock, horror, and simply, "Are you nuts?" After all, I was fifty years old and from outward appearances pretty much a typical woman who worked hard as an educator, wife, and mother within the framework set for fifty-year-old women in our society. Hiking the AT by myself did not fall into that framework. Even my mother, who had been very independent in her day, voiced concern to Uncle Marty and said, "You can't let her do that!" To which he responded, "I'm not telling her she can't do anything . . . she's her own person!" (Some insight to you about a great husband.)

I am writing this part to you because I think it's important for today's women, i.e., you and your peers, to have their own dreams and ideas and to be able to actualize them, to not be held back by what others say or think they should do. I think you already know that, but it's something that women my age and even your mom's age didn't necessarily get when we were in our twenties.

Over the last eleven years, I have talked and written about my hiking experiences in many ways. Now I'm trying to pull everything together into more than just a scrapbook or album, but something of a written documentary of my personal thoughts, conversations, and adventures as I have traveled the trail. I thought you might be a good audience for all this and that I might use letters to you as the framework for all the letters I wrote to family

and friends on the trail, to introduce various topics and to fill in the gaps of things I didn't cover in the other letters . . . so you will probably be getting many more letters from me. For now, though, I think I've written enough!

Love to you . . .
Aunt Peg

Why Do I Hike?

- The simplicity of life in the woods
- The beauty and synergy of the trees, rocks, mountains, and sky
- The in-the-moment life
- The opportunities for self-reflection
- The absence of the myriad of unimportant details in my other life
- The connection with others who think as I do about the pull of the woods . . . those for whom wildness is also a necessity
- The physical challenges which generate energy in me so that I feel alive and well in a way that my other comfortable life does not
- The inside journey it creates for me

I went into the woods
because I wished to live deliberately,
to front only the essential facts of life,
and see if I could not learn what it had to teach,
and not, when I came to die,
discover that I had not lived.

—Henry David Thoreau

A journal/log entry at Daicey Pond,
the campground/shelter just before
the final 5.7 miles to the top of Katahdin:

"There are men and women for whom the unattainable has a special attraction. Usually they are not experts: their ambitions and fantasies are strong enough to brush aside the doubts which more cautious people might have. Determination and faith are their strongest weapons. At best, such persons are regarded as eccentric; at worst, mad...

The Appalachian Trail has attracted its share of people like these. Their hiking experience varies from none at all to very slight — certainly none of them have had the kind of experience which would make a 2000 mile hike a reasonable goal. There are things they all have in common: faith in themselves, great determination and endurance."

Faith... Determination... Endurance...

     —Walt Unsworth, Everest

Dear Maria,

You asked me once when it was that I decided to hike the AT . . . I'm not sure I can give you a definitive answer on that . . . The thought of a long-distance hike on the AT floated around in my head for quite a while before I spoke out loud that I intended to actually do it. That's so typical of how I make all major decisions in my life. I mull them over, think about them, and then one day, just say it out loud to Uncle Marty or someone. Once I say it out loud, I almost always follow through.

The mulling around in my head is part of that inside journey I take in preparing for any adventure. I think about, fantasize, and discuss with myself the details of something I think I'd like to do—usually it comes after I've read or heard someone talk about an idea or an adventure that appeals to me . . . some people talk things out . . . I talk them in until I'm sure I want to do them. I guess I trust my own judgment best, so I don't seek the opinions of others as to whether or not I should do something . . . I may ask about details or how a situation was for them, just to gather information for myself, but, ultimately, I make my decision, based on what is best for me . . . and then I speak it out loud!

> ### Journal Entry: July 12, 1982
>
> Tonight Marty & I and Doug & Linda are at Cooper Brook Falls in the midst of the 100 mile wilderness on the Appalachian Trail. We've had an amazing 3 days so far. What started out as an idea to see if the 4 of us, "mid-thirtians", were still capable of handling the demands of wilderness camping has been an adventure of challenges, lively conversation, and much laughter—plus, a test of our physical abilities.
>
> Cooper Brook is lovely—the stream flows by our tents and we have had a great swim in the falls. Our lunch today was a gourmet's delight—so good, in fact, that we wrote our menu in the log book at the shelter. The feast included chicken salad (from a tin), wheat crackers, freezed dried peaches, freezed dried ice cream and lemonade.
>
> I am loving each day...being away from the "trappings" of civilization makes me wish for a longer time out here...

For the AT hike, part of the mulling in my head was fueled by a hike Uncle Marty and I took with Doug and Linda in July of 1982. We did the last seventy-five miles of the 100-mile wilderness in Maine. That was my first real backpacking trip and was quite an adventure. I'm including an excerpt from my journal in 1982 about that (you see, I was even journaling back then!). Prior to that experience, in 1974 friends of ours from Maine, Katie and Blake, hiked the AT from Georgia to New Hampshire. As they were hiking, Katie wrote a weekly column for the local newspaper in Belfast, Maine about their experiences along the trail. I was totally captivated by those columns and eagerly looked forward each week to the next installment of their adventures.

In the 1990s, I did many day and overnight hikes in Baxter Park with friends Barbara and Maggie Simon. Each time we climbed Mt. Katahdin or hiked to Russell Pond, I took a step closer to making the plan for a long-distance hike on the AT.

So in the fall of 1999, I openly talked about doing a long-distance hike the following June. In January of 2000, I started preparing with gathering gear, reading the trail books, and hiking/walking every day. In May, I remember Uncle Marty saying to me, "You actually are going to do this hike, aren't you?"

I am reminded often of the following quote from Thoreau which I'm going to include here as I believe it nicely sums up my message to you:

> If one advances confidently
> In the direction of his dreams,
> And endeavors to live the life
> Which he has imagined,
> He will meet with a success
> Unexpected in common hours.

—Henry David Thoreau

Enjoy your own inner journey and don't hesitate to speak out loud when you are ready!

Love,
Aunt Peg

Dear Maria,

I thought that this excerpt from my journal of morning pages might be a way for you to get an idea of my early yearnings to hike . . .

From all outward appearances, I appear to be an ordinary fifty-plus-year-old—perhaps more youthful looking than some of my contemporaries, but nothing physical in dress or accoutrements that would suggest that I was one who didn't fit with the mainstream of women my age. It has been that way my whole life. Quiet and shy as a young girl and then a teenager, there was nothing to mark me as different except perhaps an air of confidence that was budding or independence in the making. Certainly I was not the athletic type or seemingly, the outdoors type. I didn't talk about how I loved the outdoors, loved camping, or how important nature seemed to me. Actually, looking back, I'm not sure that I knew those things about myself either—but they were brewing . . . As I read *Heidi* or other stories about living in the mountains or wilderness, I found myself romanticizing those lifestyles . . . that was probably the beginning of a fantasy life which, over time, developed fully in my head . . . my inside journey I call it. I didn't share that life in my head with anyone; it was what I carried around, retreating to it periodically, adding to it as I read more and more; all that was before it became clear to me that I could actualize my dreams. That life remained just a dream for many years . . . perhaps I thought that if I shared it with other people, they'd make fun of me or tell me they couldn't imagine me doing that.

There's that whole idea of the inside journey again! Now that I've labeled it, it seems to be at the heart of what helps me figure out the things I want to do.

Love,
Aunt Peg

9/ 2002

Dear Rainy & Victor,

It's about 5 pm and I am sitting on the "deck" of a shelter – all I can see are beautiful trees with late afternoon sun shining through – There are all kinds of interesting sounds, mostly birds, I assume

I should just put this out there: I hike because of days and moments like now – the weather has been perfect – the trees, rocks, mountains, sky all blend together to create a backdrop for a walk in the woods which is a totally mystical, spiritual, soothing journey – I am loving my time by myself & I am totally comfortable & happy

Hope all is well with you –

♡ Peggy

RAINY

June 13, 2000

Dear Jill,

This is day 4 and I really feel like I've entered another world! Right now it's 4:30 PM and I am in a shelter with 3 other people in a very beautiful spot — huge pine trees, a great book and everything green — and it's pouring cold rain!

This is a far cry from my life in the school system! Interestingly, though, even among some hikers there is the challenge, "How far can I go today?" and they race up/down the trail, proving how fast they can go but missing the beautiful spots. Already I have abandoned that carefully created itinerary I made. These first few days I have hiked slowly, partially to minimize the shock on my body of the 40 lb. pack I'm carrying. That's way too much and tomorrow I'll be in Salesbury so I'll go to the Post office and send stuff home.

RAINY

I've decided² to hike slowly if I want, fast when I want, and to take a break anytime I want! The first day was 100° and I had a tough time. I found myself thinking "What strategies can I use to get up these hills more easily." Then I decided to forget the "strategies" — I would do it slowly with as many breaks as I needed — I have kept, however, the strategy of cheering positively whenever I approach a really steep section, ie. "Yea! Another steep part!" — thinking that a positive approach will make it easier! — At any rate, please know that if you & Mike join me, it'll be a leisurely walk, not a race!

♡ Peggy

9/2008

Dear Martha,

I was thinking about our conversation recently where we talked about the lure of a good hike up/over a mountain so I know you'll identify with this thought of mine — it seems that the physical challenges of hiking really generate such energy for me — much more than anything I might do in my "other" life which is, of course, much more comfortable (or maybe "comfortable" is the operative word here!). Probably being 60+ has something to do with why I feel so compelled to tackle a tough climb or a long hike — I do need to be able to answer my own question of "How physically fit am I anyway?".

Since we share the same "gene source", perhaps it's similar for you —

♡ Peg

May, 2006

Dear Suz,

. Well, here I am — back on the AT again! . This time it's just for a week, but I'm loving being back. There are quite a few hikers out here — mostly my age or older (it's the time of year! — you have to be retired). Few women, though. It's funny how easily connections are made with other hikers; in addition to all the other reasons I love to hike, I realize that those connections are important to me — probably because we feel the same about being in the woods! The conversations along the trail are usually about the beauty around us or the challenges or the animals ...

I was reminded today that in 2004 Maggie + I hiked through the presidential election! Never once did we discuss election issues along the trail or at night; the most said was that we all agreed we were glad to be missing the television coverage, ads + hoopla accompanying the campaigns. On election day we happened to cross a road + person in a parked car announced to us that Bush had won. We "took note" + moved on! That's what I love about being out here —

Love, Peg

Dear Jill,   6/2000
Today was a beautiful day for
hiking — the sky was bright blue, temps
were 72° with a breeze and no
humidity — at any rate, I'm finally
in a rhythm of hiking where I can
actually think about things) other
than "how high is this hill?" and
"Why won't my blister stop hurting?"
I spent the morning trying to sort
out why this whole trip has been a
personal goal for me — I came to
the conclusion that there are
many factors) that played into
making it important for me to do
this. I have always (since I was
a little girl + read the book Heidi)
found the idea of a simple life
outdoors) intriguing. In many
ways I have often felt that I
didn't quite "fit" into the life
in Maryland that so many
people my age have — so I guess,
if I don't quite fit, then I'll
be sure to do things) to show
how different I am!

APPALACHIAN
TRAIL
CROSSING
AHEAD

RAINY

Dear Maggie,

    I have been thinking about where our "hiking genes" come from, particularly since recently when I was reading Nana Philbrook's journals (your great grandmother), I came across an entry in 1936 which simply said, "Marion climbed Mt. Washington today." Thinking that there must have been another Mt. Washington, I called Mom (your Nana) and asked her. She said, "Oh yes... I climbed up on skis and then skied down. You know that picture of me on skis, well that was taken by Robert Hanscom that day." Needless to say, I was shocked. Mom's initial reaction to my hiking made me think that she had no idea how exciting or

6/2000

exhilarating it could be to be on top of a mountain or to hike long distances. The summer I reached the top of Mt. Washington on the AT, I called her from a pay phone + she listened as I enthusiastically described what I could see + what it felt like to be on top of such a high mountain. I had no idea that she herself had been there at a much younger age!

Of course I had always thought that I got my love of hiking + the outdoors from my dad (your grandad) - you know the stories of him as a Maine Guide and the long walks in the woods with him pointing out where a moose had been or where a deer had spent the night, where the eagle lived, etc. I'm sorry he didn't live long enough to know of us hiking together on the AT – he'd have loved that!

Anyway – it seems that perhaps our love of the outdoors, climbing, and hiking comes from both my parents/your grandparents. It's in our blood so no wonder we can't get enough of it!

Love,
aunt Peg

Dear Pat,   7/2003
        I have to tell you about a conver-
sation that was totally surprising to me!
You know the people involved so I thought
you'd get a chuckle out of it - last fall
Searsport had a reunion for several
classes. I wasn't able to go, but my sister Martha went. When she had conversation with Victor & Dale, she told them
about me hiking the AT by myself—
Victor's reply, "That's not the Peggy Alden
I knew!" was what shocked me!
        I guess that while it had been clear
to me that I would eventually hike a
long distance, I never really talked about
it to others until the time was near—so
others just didn't know about it.
        Anyway, to his credit, when I later
questioned Victor about his comment, he
redeemed himself by saying, "you knew
when I thought about it, I remembered
that you were the one who climbed Mt.
Battie with me in the dark—that should
have been my clue!"
        So, Pat—I'm wondering if I ever
really talked to you about hiking??
I'd be curious to know! ♡ Peg

10/2004
Great Smokies!

Dear Fara,

 As I was hiking this AM I was reminded of our conversation last summer about whether or not I'd done extensive hiking as a young person — of course I had done "car camping" with my family, but, otherwise, I knew no one else who talked about hiking, camping, climbing mountains, living outside for days on end... Had I been a teenager or college student in these days, it'd been different, I'm sure.. but, in the 50's + 60's I wasn't a part of any group who considered doing anything like that — we were driven by school + school activities — following the "protocol" of good kids who did "normal" things!! Not that there was anything wrong with hiking, camping, mountain climbing, but it just wasn't in the framework of what we did wholeheartedly — we only dabbled in it...I climbed Mt. Battie, I skied, I took walks, I read — I fantasized in my head about hiking + climbing! all that swirled around in my head for many years... then I finally spoke out loud that I wanted to hike and it became a possibility! ...and here I am — in the midst of an incredible hike in the Great Smoky Mtns — yes — this is the good life!! — Hope all is well.
♡ Peggy

Jill,   6/2000
    Just a quick note to "add to" my
initial letter of why I'm doing this
hike!
    I am NOT doing this trip because
I have to sort out my life—I
think I do that pretty regularly anyway...but, I do think another reason
I am doing it, though, is to have time to
be in the moment, to stop + start as I
wish, to indulge in a very simple life,
and to concentrate only on myself.
In some respects, it's a pretty selfish
thing I'm doing—but, I've gotten
over that! I do feel fortunate
that those in my life who depend
on me have been so encouraging +
supportive...
    Do my ramblings make any
sense?!! More another time—
        ♡ P.

RAINY

June 19, 2000

Dear Barb + Mags (I know Nalan is in Maine),

Well, here I am in the woods in Massachusettes. So far its a great adventure! I think about you guys all the time because all the hiking and camping we did together has really prepared me for this. The 2nd day out I had to ford a stream (one very similar to the one on route to Russell Pond!) and I did it with no problems! Having my water sandals with me was helpful! There's been a ton of rain so of course wet, sloppy trails — but never so bad as that trip back from Russell Pond (I think I knew then that I would forever gauge how bad other "rain" was by that day!!). Also, the bugs are out and about, but never as bad as that night on the Zen trip with Dana — remember trying to eat dinner with thousands of mosquitoes? — Also, sleeping in a lean-to with 3 men is no sweat after having done it on the Zen trip! Early on I was thinking about how and when the idea of hiking the AT became something I really wanted to do — I think I pinned it down to a book you gave me, Barb, years ago — we still have at camp — Springer Mtn. to Katahdin — I think that's when I first hatched the idea of wanting to do this —

Journal Entry, 1996: The Zen Camping Trip

For the past 4 days Barb, Maggie, and I have been on an incredible backpacking/hiking trip to Black Mountain led by a professor at Univ. Maine in Portland. We were given a list of what to bring: backpack, sleeping bag, clothing as well as what not to bring: paper/pen, books, watches, our last names, our "other" lives! Dana (the professor) provided the food, tents, and the leadership. There were 6 of us (7 including Dana)—4 men and the 3 of us women.

The trip was designed to give us opportunities to be outside in the wilderness and to learn from Dana about Zen Buddhism. The goal was to practice being in the moment, hence the no last names, no talk about what we did in our "other" lives, no watches, etc. The days and evenings were filled with interesting philosophical conversations, chanting, meditating along with a great hike in the woods.

This was my first dip into understanding the concepts of "being in the moment" and Buddhism, as they applied to my place in nature.......

Dear Maria,

"Wildness is a necessity," so says John Muir. I love his approach to the outdoors! As soon as I heard that quote, I knew it described what a part of me had been thinking but that I couldn't put my finger on . . . that wildness he talks about is the essence of what I feel when I am out in the woods hiking . . . it's the freedom from society's imprint, the simple lifestyle that comes from carrying everything you need on your back, the lack of other world disruptions to your thoughts, the absence of day-to-day concerns, discussions, worries . . . the wildness, in spite of what is conjured up by the word wild, is really the calmness and clarity that comes from opportunities to be still, to reflect, to think about my place in nature, and to get to know  myself, my needs, and desires without the contamination of the expectations of a society whose values may not be in sync with mine. I find that I always emerge from the woods clearheaded and very present in the moment, but not always in concert with the hectic pace of life which so many people today live.

My urges to hike are really based on when I know I have had enough of the markers of a society where the nightly news displays and emphasizes the negative aspects of community life and local and world politics; where traffic, noise, and pollution disrupt daily routines; and where petty worries define the conversation among people. It is always clear to me when I need to be back out on the trail.

Well, Maria, I've certainly rambled on about this, but I hope it makes sense to you in the context of why I hike . . . perhaps this whole notion resonates with you as well.

Love,
Aunt Peg

WHAT ARE THE DETAILS OF MY HIKES?

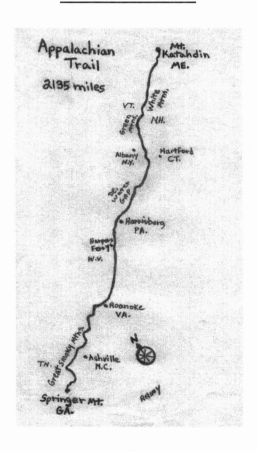

The trail is a fluid experience . . .

Dear Maria,

Re: My AT hikes 2000-2010

It occurred to me that my letters in this book could be confusing as I've not put them in chronological order! I have tried to group them according to topics and, in doing so, often there is a letter from 2000 alongside of one from 2004 . . . so, I decided to make a list of my hikes in chronological order of their dates and where they were . . . just so, if you are inclined, you can determine which letters go with which hikes! You will notice that sometimes I have hiked sections more than once; usually that is when others have joined me and have wanted to do a particular part.

Love,
Aunt Peg

My AT Hikes, 2000-2010

- 1997-2000: Day trips to parts of the trail in West Virginia, Maryland, and Pennsylvania

- June 2000-August 2000: New York/Connecticut line to Mt. Katahdin, Maine

- July 2001: The Bigelow Mountains in Maine

- August 2001: A section in southern Maine

- September 2002: Northern Virginia through Shenandoah National Park to Waynesboro, Virginia

- September-November 2004: Central Virginia to Springer Mountain, Georgia

- September 2005 Sections in Virginia and Tennessee

- May 2006: Waynesboro, Virginia, to Tye River, Virginia

- August 2006: Caratunk to Bigelow Mountains, Maine

- March 2008: Winter camping/hiking, Baxter State Park, Maine

- May 2008: Tye River to James River, Virginia

- September 2008: 100-mile wilderness, Maine

- May 2009: Pennsylvania line to Harper's Ferry, western Virginia (the Maryland Section)

- September 2009: 100-mile wilderness, Maine

- April 2010: New York to New Jersey/Pennsylvania line

July 25, 2000

Dear Carolyn & John,

Greetings from the Maine woods! Right now I'm sitting in my tent after a long day of perfect hiking — the weather was in the 70's, no humidity, blue sky & sun, a 14 mile stretch of mostly even terrain with one fairly easy mountain! I'm having a wonderful time and all is going well.

I am enjoying being outdoors and in the woods every day — the hiking at times has been challenging, other times (like today) very easy. Climbing in the White Mountains was great — steep & rocky, but the 25 mile trek across the tops of the Presidential range was absolutely spectacular. I was so fortunate to have good weather for that. When I was doing that section I stayed in huts all along the way, up in the mountains. That was fun. + I was able to carry a lighter

pack because I didn't take my tent, stove, pots, etc. The huts have co-ed bunkrooms, a big dining area + indoor toilets (no showers, no electricity). The "crew" served breakfast and dinner so that was a nice break from cooking on my little stove every night.

This weekend I'll meet my friend Darcy in Monson, Maine + we will start the "100 mile wilderness" — it'll be fun to have her along for that.

One of the surprises on this trip is how social + tight knit the trail community (thru hikers + long distance section hikers) is. Even though I am hiking alone, I have made many friends + I run into people I've met almost every day. Everyone uses a Trail name (mine is Blueberry) and no one really talks about their "other lives" so it is as though

everyone is equal out here. I did meet 2 women who were out for 10 days — They are in their 40's + we camped together one night — we did trade stories of our "other lives" + we really clicked. Next year I am going to hike with them for their annual trip. They've been sending me packages, books, etc. since I saw them in June!

— Well — all for now — Hope you are having a good summer —

Peggy

October 1, 2004

Dear Marty,

Thought I'd drop you a note before you head to Maine — we'll be at the hostel tomorrow & hopefully, I'll mail this!

We've had good hiking since Damascus. Maggie's feet are doing well & actually yesterday we doubled our mileage, going 16 miles instead of 8. The first night out of Damascus we were at the shelter with 3 of the Damascus friends — Niko, Pisses & Kevin. They made a big bonfire which was nice & we sat around sipping brandy (one) & whiskey (the others). The only thing missing was you! I know you'd have loved it! Later that night I was asleep in my tent & Niko called to me, "Blueberry, come out — you've got to see this incredible moon!" It was a beautiful, totally full moon & I was glad he called to me to see it.

When Maggie & I left on Wednesday we stopped by the Outfitters one more time — to have our packs weighed — mine was 50 lbs. — hers 47!! I am really trying to work on reducing that

-2-

weight — It's only supposed to be 1/3 of your body weight so 50 is way too much — Niko, of course, said, "You are two powerful women!"

Tonight we are at a shelter that is full so Maggie is going to sleep in the tent with me. There are Kevin, 2 older men, and a couple who are out here celebrating their 12th anniversary (she is wearing a skirt!)

So often there is no one at the shelters — this seems a little strange!

♡ Peg

July 2, 2000

Dear Sara & Bill,

Greetings from somewhere in Vermont! Today I hiked through a gorgeous section - way up high through a pine forest. It smelled like a Christmas tree shop!

What has been a pleasant surprise for me on this hike has been the "friendliness of the "Trail Community, ie. all the thru-hikers & long distance section hikers - There's a whole sub-culture in this trail community which is intriguing - complete with its own language, rules, issues & concerns!

Everyone uses a trail name instead of their real name - It's easy to remember the people you meet because the trail name is usually based on a unique characteristic for the person - There are many interesting people I've met, including Gypsy, Father Time, Mother Goose, Shadow, Songbird, Journeyman, Dreamer, etc. My name is Blueberry (picked by Marty)-

-2-

must say I initially felt a little silly introducing myself that way, but now it's a habit!

. Other specific language includes terms like: slack packing*, yellow blazing*, zero days*, Nobo's*, Sobo's*, etc.!

There is Trail Magic* which is pretty neat — like the concept of Random Acts of Kindness... the other day I found chocolate candy on top of my pack which someone had left for me. Sometimes in the middle of the woods, you'll find a cooler of cold sodas or cookies + snacks hanging from a bag in a tree.

There are a few rules — actually, only 2 that are posted:
• Carry in, carry out, leave no trace — this is huge among thru-hikers + long distance hikers. It's frustrating when day hikers don't get this "concept."
• Don't pee in the privy! That makes me laugh whenever I think about it. This is posted when the privys are composting toilets — they claim that "pee" makes them smell so we should just use the woods.

So, this is what the culture looks like, but, most importantly, everyone has the same goal: To hike the trail + enjoy it + to do the hike Your way, not someone else's way! ♡ Peggy

July 6, 2000

Dear Diane + Jim,

Thank you so much for the great care package! I was in Killington, VT over the 4th so got my mail yesterday. The power bars are great — as you can imagine, I'm eating a ton of food + am always having to stock up on power bars. I carry M+M's in my pocket (did I tell you that?) so the ones you sent were consumed today! Plus, I sprinkled the package of seeds in a field I passed through today — what fun it is to think of creating wildflowers.

You asked if I was tired — actually NO — because I get more sleep now than when I am home in my "other life." All long distance hikers are diligent about sleeping + eating. Everyone is usually asleep by 8:30 – 9:00 and then up around 6:00 so that's 8-9 hours of sleep each night.

I didn't go into this trip with the thought of making a lot of friends, but I have, in fact, met many wonderful people — it's all a big network out here. As a matter of fact, a guy just came into the shelter + said, "Are you Blueberry?" He then said, "Elderberry (a 68 year old lady) said to tell you she'll be along soon!"

—2—

Marty is meeting me tomorrow for the weekend which I'm looking forward to greatly. He will bring my warm clothes for hiking the White Mtns. (which I'm starting on Sunday) & will take my tent, stove, etc. so I can carry a lighter pack over the mountains. I will stay in huts each night for 5 nights which will be a nice change — There are bunks, an indoor bathroom (although no showers or hot water) & breakfast & dinner each day — for a price, of course! The kids who are hiking usually "work" to stay there, but I'm splurging & will enjoy the "luxury" a bit.

Today has been beautiful — sunny, but cool — Right now there are 4 of us here, reading & writing. Soon it'll be time to get dinner & maybe have a fire (there is a nice firepit at this shelter & some dry wood) — Then, off to bed! I have only 7 miles to go to meet Marty tomorrow so it'll be a leisurely hike —

Take care — hope your trip to the Alps was great!

Love,
Peggy

9/16/02
Virginia

Dear Jill,

Well... here I am back on the AT! This is the 2nd night out & I'm doing the same thing with letters this time so please save this & return it, please!

Tonight I am at a "luxury" shelter which has a porch, bunk beds & even an outdoor shower, plus water from a spring which comes out of a faucet!! It's called the Denton Shelter (in honor of a couple, Jim + Molly Denton, who've devoted their lives to working on the AT.) I got here around 3 & thought I'd be by myself as I've seen very few hikers (no women) but a young man just came & it turns out he's from Union, Maine — not far from Searsport & Swan Lake — what a small world! He said he knew I'd be here because I'd signed in at the last shelter when I ate lunch & then he ran into 4 men whom I'd also chatted with & they told him I was headed this way. — What a funny networking system there is out here!

Everything is really wet now because we had a sudden shower just a mile before I got here. Luckily the sun has come out & I've spread everything out to dry.

Marty is coming on Wednesday — he'll meet me in Shenandoah Nat'l Park & we'll camp at a regular campground in our big tent Wed + Thurs. That'll be nice! Then on Saturday, my friend Diane Rausch will meet me in the AM — we'll hike Saturday & then stay in a lodge in the park Sat. night. She has never hiked before but has been very interested in this and is going to give it a try — but she didn't want to sleep in a tent, so conveniently there is a lodge in the park & we'll go right by it on the AT!

All for now — ♡ Peggy

Day 10 – NY
Rainy

May 3, 2010

Dear Doug + Linda,

Greetings from the AT! – Actually,
today I'm in a little trail community –
Greenwood Lake, NY. I needed to re-supply
+ also to get clean so decided to come
into this town + spend the night. This
is all part of the trail life – finding the
little communities along the way which
are "hiker friendly" – That information is
passed from hiker to hiker + sometimes
is included in the AT companion book.

This 15 day trip has been a microcosm
of the 2 big hikes I've taken – I'm doing
it alone + have deliberately worked at
taking things at a slow pace – stopping

for long lunch breaks, stopping to listen to the birds, stopping at all the viewpoints. The weather has been totally variable — perfect, then cold + rainy w/ a few snowflakes, then 80°-90° + today rain with 70° temps - ??! I do poorest in the 80°-90° temps with humidity — another reminder to me of why we don't live in Maryland in the summer!

As always, I've met unusual characters — although not many people are out here at this time of the year — No women so far — and, the most interesting question I've gotten (3 x's) is "How old are you?" I'm not sure what to make of that?!!

I conceded to bringing my cell phone with me this time + have actually enjoyed having it (I have it turned off except for when I need to call) and Marty + I are able to talk each night which is nice.

I'll be home 5/9 & will be in touch then — Take care — Love, Peg
PS Save this & send it back please

10 miles
Rainy in the AM
Warm sun in
the PM
Windy & chilly
tonight!

4/27/2010
New York

Dear Stan & Carol,
Greetings from the AT! This is Day 4
of the two week trip & so far all is well.
As it turned out, my friend Brigid was
not able to come because of an emergency
with her daughter in Denver—so Friday
I drove her car from DC to Connecticut &
stayed in her house before starting the
hike on Saturday. A friend of hers took
me to the trailhead at Hoyt Rd near Kent, CT.
In 2000 that also was where we started the
first hike only going North to Maine—this
time I headed south into NY. You'd think
finding the AT trailhead would be easy,
however, I always have trouble finding
it & this was no exception — Marty & I had the
same trouble 10 years ago - it's always on

some obscure back road, poorly marked!
This is a beautiful time of year to hike as the trees are just leafing, wildflowers are everywhere + the trail is very uncrouded - So far I've only encountered one other woman who is section hiking like I am. On the weekend there were some day hikers + 1 night hikers, but during the week there are very few. 3 miles into the N Y section is a metro stop - called "Appalachian Trail stop" so people can actually come out from NY City for a day or overnight hike using the metro. In spite of that there is nothing else of the hustle bustle of New York City out here at all. The landscapes I see from the trail are farms, meadows + hills - I've hiked through 3 fields already where there are actual cows! The trail in the woods is lined with the huge rock formations that mark the trail in every state. Yesterday + today I hiked through forests w the huge old trees which are beautiful.
The last two nights I've stayed in shelters but tonight I'm in my tent. It rained terribly Sunday + Monday + all my gear got wet - so I was happy to see the sun today + most everything has dried. Thursday night I'll stay in Bear Mtn. Inn - so will have a shower, real bed + a meal in a restaurant! - Then it'll be back to camping again - Well, I'm out of room - Please send this back to me! Thanks
Love, Peggy

Day 5
8.5 miles
cold, sunny+
windy
NY

4/28/2010

Dear Doug + Bev,

Greetings from the AT! Tonight I am in, what might appear, a very unlikely place! — I'm staying in the Hiker Shelter in the ballpark at the Franciscan Monastery—Graymoor in New York! They have encouraged hikers to stay in their shelter since 1972 & in the past have even invited hikers to eat with them (not now, though). This order was founded by St. Francis of Assisi in the 1200's & is noted for hospitality to strangers. It is right on the trail so a perfect place to stay. I do, however, think of Doug Behrens' comment when we & were canoeing the Allagash in Maine. He said, "I'm 40 years old and am sleeping in the mud (exaggeration) on a river bank in Northern Maine. This is what I'm doing for my vacation?!" So I thought, "I'm 63 years old +

am sleeping on the concrete floor of a picnic shelter in 30° weather!" —But, it's part of the hiking life—that other life I lead sometimes & I love it.

I think I mentioned to you that those two states—N Y & N J (162 miles total) are the last ones to complete the whole 2100 mile trek for me. Ironically, 10 years ago when I started, I ~~stay~~ started in Hoyt, Conn. at a trail head & hiked North to Maine. This time I started at the same trail head & am headed south.

New York has been beautiful—when you go to the interior of the woods, it looks like what you see in children's books about animals who live in the woods or like The Hobbit, etc. Since I don't wear my glasses when I hike, my long distance vision is compromised & everything I see at a distance looks like a fantasy animal! Today I passed by a tree which could have been a model for a high rise apartment building (for birds)

Holes designating different apartments!

entry with many nut shells—perhaps the "dining room —

The weather has been very cold (snow flurries last night), windy, & rainy—Tomorrow is supposed to be better. I wear all my clothes to bed to keep warm — Must close—Please save letter. Hope you're all OK.

Love, Peggy

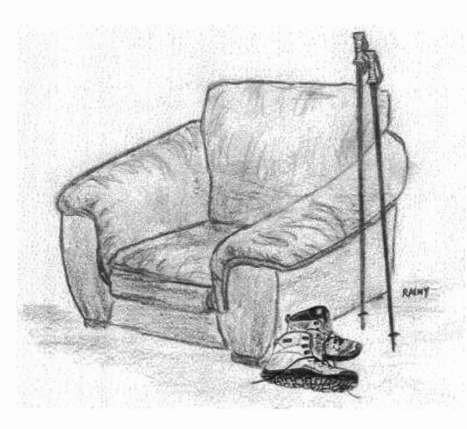

The Armchair Hiker

Who Are My Friends on the Trail?

My niece, Maggie, is a perfect hiking partner! We can finish each other's sentences, think the same thoughts —She's comfortable + easy to be with — I've obviously known her all my life/her life but hiking together takes our relationship to a new dimension — 10/04

Darcy Rollins (daughter of our friends in Maine) is with me, hiking the last 100 miles. We're having a great time — wonderful conversation + trail comraderie. We'll be at Mt. Katahdin on August 10th! 8/2000

Well, a couple of women have showed up to share this campsite — They are out for 2 weeks + have a dog. It's nice to have company + they seem like fun — 6/2000

On the trail, you live for right now with the people you meet . . .

Dear Maria,

Re: Hiking companions

You've heard me talk about many of the people I've met on the trail, so I thought I'd tell you a bit about meeting people and how sometimes they become my friends!

First, though, I should remind you that initially I started hiking the AT alone and had no idea I'd develop friendships along the way. I have always loved the chances to be by myself in the woods with time to think and reflect . . . but then I have also discovered the joys of companionship on the trail.

For any long-distance hiker, there are opportunities daily to connect with other hikers. Protocol on the trail suggests that hikers stop and chat when meeting on the trail, even if for just a minute or so. Much valuable information is passed that way, e.g., "I saw a big black bear just ten minutes from here" or "I heard we're in for a huge thunderstorm later this morning . . ." Just the connection with others who are doing what you are doing is energizing.

Often, I'll find repeat encounters with the same hikers, particularly if they are on the same hiking itinerary as I am. I don't usually hike with someone I've just met, but if we see each other night after night at the same shelter, share stories and AT experiences, a friendship is often forged and sometimes continues long after the hike.

On my hike in 2000, one night I was camping alone in a spot in Massachusetts when suddenly I heard a lot of loud conversation and laughter coming from the trail headed south (I was headed north). Two women fairly close to my age and a dog appeared at the site to set up for the night . . . with the opening comment, "We hope you don't mind, but we are very chatty!" Recently, eight years and several hiking trips with them later, we have just returned from doing a section in the 100-mile wilderness and a climb of Mt. Katahdin!

Laurie (Sweet Patooty) from Georgia, Brigid (Tooty) from Connecticut, and I began a friendship that night which continues today! We meet at least twice a year for a five—to seven-day hike on the AT. Between hikes we keep in touch by e-mail or phone. Our trips always include some spontaneous adventure which takes us away from our plan and gives us many opportunities to laugh until we cry!

I'm including a letter about a recent adventure with them so you can see what I mean—

More later . . .

Love,
Aunt Peg

RAINY

Dear Suz,   9/14/08
    I'm writing from the AT
this morning so please save
this and return it so it'll be
part of my "letters from the AT"
book!
    We left on Wednesday - Laurie,
Brigid and I. Marty drove us
to the trailhead - about 26
miles from Katahdin in
the 100 mile wilderness.* As
always, it's been an incredible
hike - full of unexpected adventures, great hiking plus much
laughter and trail comraderie.
    Yesterday we took a side
trail off the AT to Pemadumcook
lake where we blew a horn
(attached to a tree!) and a
guy in a boat drove over from
across the lake at White

-2-
House Landing (a fishing lodge) to
pick us up - He took us to the
lodge where we spent the night
in a bunk house with 40 others.
There were also 4 or 5 other hikers
in a cottage so it was a lively
group. The people who own
the place are great and we
had cheeseburgers, pizza, homemade apple pie for dinner
along with any kind of Ben
+ Jerry's ice cream we wanted!
This morning they made bacon,
eggs, English muffins + blueberry
pancakes for everyone for breakfast. It was so good to have
non-trail food + the company
was very fun. We play a dice
game called Farkle* when

57

-3-

we hike so we taught that to everyone last night.

This morning was another adventure as we decided. we needed to "move up" 22 miles to meet our deadline of climbing Katahdin on Tuesday so we hired a seaplane to pick us up at White House Landing's pier & he flew the 3 of us up to another lake on the AT — 22 miles ahead! It was a great spontaneous idea that worked! When we got into the plane, the other hikers were on the pier taking pictures of it all! We felt like celebrities!! — We ended up hiking 9 miles after we got out at the next lake. — so are now ready for Katahdin on Tuesday after 14 miles tomorrow.

Must go to bed now — More later

Love, Peg

Dear Maria,

Re: More about hiking companions!

I have been fortunate to meet such incredible people on the AT. I'm writing today about Brenda and Reggie, a.k.a. the Carolina Creepers. When I hiked the section in the White Mountains in 2000, I met them. They were traveling the same route and staying at the same huts as I was. We became fast friends and while we didn't hike together during the day, we spent much time in the evenings swapping life stories and hiking experiences. They had spent a number of years hiking the trail, one state at a time; I joined them the next year (2001) for a section in Maine when they were finally completing the trail.

In 2004, when I finished my two-month hike at Springer Mountain in Georgia, they surprised me by driving all the way from South Carolina to celebrate the end of that trip with me.

We still keep in touch via e-mail and an occasional phone call—friends you bond with on the trail are forever in your heart!

Enough for now . . .

♡ aunt Peg

The Sun : Sunday, December 10, 2000 : Page 3ʀ

PERSONAL JOURNEYS

A MEMORABLE PLACE

Friendships on the trail

By PEGGY STOUT
SPECIAL TO THE SUN

In the midst of my two-month journey hiking the Appalachian Trail from New York to Maine this summer, climbing the magnificent White Mountains of New Hampshire and staying in the "hut" system seemed like a vacation within a vacation.

As I approached the White Mountains, my husband met me in Franconia Notch, N.H., the first leg of the Presidential Range. Recognizing the unpredictability of the weather in that region, especially above the tree line. I decided to leave my tent, stove, cooking utensils and food with my husband in exchange for some warmer clothing and reservations to stay at six of the 10 huts managed by the Appalachian Mountain Club in New Hampshire.

The huts are positioned a day's hike apart along the trail and are accessible by side trails for weekend hikers as well as those going longer distances. Resembling old-fashioned schoolhouses, the buildings

Mountain high: Lake of the Clouds hut is a half-mile from Mount Washington.

vary in size (accommodations range from 30 to 90 people) and personality, but all include one or more large bunkrooms (with bunks stacked four high), indoor bathrooms (no showers) and a large family/dining room with long tables for game playing, socializing, reading, writing and, of course, eating. Breakfast and dinner are incredible meals cooked and served family style by a friendly staff of mostly college students.

Having just completed nearly a month of hiking on my own, sleeping

in my tent and carrying minimal amounts of food, I found myself enjoying the luxuries of beds and blankets, indoor plumbing and the delightful meals prepared for me. But I also became immersed in my group of new friends, many of whom were traveling the same route as I for the same amount of time.

We did not necessarily hike together, but we usually left at the same time in the morning, sometimes had lunch together on the trail and often reunited at the next hut later that day.

In the evenings, we swapped hiking stories, plans and dreams, speculated on who might snore in the bunkroom that night, watched sunsets together and sat and soaked our feet in waterfalls and streams. In short, we quickly developed friendships.

In addition to the challenges of climbing, as well as witnessing the breathtaking panoramas of mountains, "hiking the huts" provided much more than I anticipated: good food, entertainment and a real sense of camaraderie.

Peggy Stout lives in Finksburg.

This is an article I wrote for the Baltimore Sun; Brenda & Reggie were the inspirations for this . . .

Dear Maria,

Re: Even more about hiking companions!

During my first long-distance hike in 2000, for the section known as the 100-mile wilderness* (the last section in Maine before climbing Katahdin), my friend Darcy joined me. Young and athletic from high school and college days, Darcy, a.k.a. Sal, was a great hiking companion. I have known her since she was born as her parents are longtime friends of mine. This, however, was an opportunity to get to know her on a different level. As we hiked, we spent countless hours talking about every issue there was to discuss. It was refreshing for me and very enjoyable after a month and a half by myself to have stimulating conversation and a chance to get to know Darcy as her own person, not the little girl I had watched grow up.

Love,
Aunt Peg

Dear Maria,

Re: More about hiking companions/another niece!

In 2004, when I was getting organized to do another two-month hike, my niece Maggie (from Maine) approached me and said she'd like to hike with me. She was twenty-two and had recently graduated from college (same spot as you are now); she thought that being out in the woods would be a good way for her to reflect on her next move in life (sound familiar?).

Hiking with Maggie, a.k.a. Friend, for two months allowed me to see life on the trail through another perspective, one which perhaps I had once but lost for many years . . . and now have recaptured, thanks to her! I find that hiking with others who are much younger than I, especially women, helps me to step out of myself and view the world differently. One of the things that I have learned through hiking is that we often get stuck in one way of thinking or looking at things. Having an opportunity to be out of that paradigm and into another for a period of time is energizing, liberating, and, basically, plain refreshing!

More later . . . .

♡ aunt Peg

Dear Maria,

Re: More hiking companions!

During the 2004, hike Maggie and I became good friends with hikers English Stu (a contemporary of mine from England who retired from his job, turned sixty, flew to the U.S. and started on the AT in Daleville, Virginia, all in the same week!) and Niko, a thirty-plus young man who had life stories, conversation, and humor which kept us constantly entertained.

Well into that hike, Laurie, a.k.a. Sweet Patooty, joined us for a week which added new energy to the group. Laurie always brings laughter and good conversation to a situation which we all particularly appreciated at that point in our hike.

Over the years of hiking, there have been many others I've met or taken with me on short hikes. I've enjoyed them, as well. While it's not always possible to stay in touch with these folks, I do remember them through conversations we had and experiences we shared.

Love,
Aunt Peg

6/15/2000

Dear Marcella, Joe, Joey + Chris,

Here I am in a totally different world! Tonight I'm camping in a beautiful spot next to waterfalls + a stream (if it were not so cold, I'd have a shower in the falls!) There are huge pine trees, big boulders + an incredible view. It's been a great hike so far although it has rained almost every day, sometimes very hard! Usually I try to camp near a shelter (lean-to) so that if it rains hard I can go into that. The other night there were four of us in the shelter plus a mother bird who was sitting on her nest in the rafters (she was none too happy with us!).

I've met many other long distance hikers — few women — but a number of men Jeff's age and then some who are more my age. The interesting thing about conversations with the other hikers is that one never really talks about his/her "other" life. It's

-2-

always about places on the trail, where they've been, where they're going, what they've seen, etc.

One young ridge runner* (an AT employee who hikes a section to be sure all is well) hiked a while with me. He was 23 — he told me that after I told him my son was 23; anyway, he was curious about people's reactions to me doing this — When he asked me what my husband thought + was he "worried"? I said, "yes, he was worried, but he was also very supportive," and he replied in a sweet way, "He wouldn't be a good husband if he didn't worry, but please tell him there's no need to worry!" That comment certainly endeared him to me!!

♡ Peggy

June 28, 2000

Dear Pete + Barbara,
   I thought I'd try to send this to you so it'd arrive just before the 4th of July — you know I'll be thinking of all of you that day. I will be somewhere in the Vermont woods on the 4th + will probably be wishing I had some of your strawberry shortcake! At any rate, be sure to tell everyone I said hello.
   I'm having a great trip, full of interesting adventures! Tonight I am sleeping in the Eco-Center on top of Mt. Stratton Ski area — Tomorrow I have to pick up a package of supplies from Marty + that means getting down the mountain to the village. Some guys who are working up here on a bird project suggested I stay here + take the gondola down + back tomorrow —
   Yesterday I hiked 8 miles in torrential rain, but this morning I woke up to a perfectly gorgeous day — blue sky, temps about 72°, a little breeze, no humidity — that is a perfect hiking day.
   There are many interesting people hiking the trail. I met one guy from Tennessee who is a 4th grade teacher. He took a semester leave of absence + is

RAINY

-2-

a thru-hiker. Before he left, he taught his students all about the Appalachian Mtns, the trail, etc. and then created an interactive website – he carries a little laptop + everyday kids write questions to him + he responds! He also carried a journal + asked everyone he met to write something about hiking to his students.

Last night I stayed at a shelter with a mother (who's a kindergarten teacher) and her 4 kids ranging from age 7-12. They'll be hiking all summer also, but on the Long Trail which goes through Vermont to Canada. For about 75 miles, the Long Trail & the AT follow the same route.

I hope you're having a good summer – I do miss the lake & all the regular summer activities, but I am loving life on the trail right now!

Love, Peggy

Day 26   10/5/04
Cherry Gap Shelter
Sunny - 60°
8.7 miles

Dear Mom & Mary,
     All is fine with us! Maggie's feet
have had the miracle cure - new inserts
in her boots. We are having a wonderful
hike - yesterday & today we have been
hiking on the Tennessee - North Carolina
border so we never are quite sure which
state we are in - It's beautiful,
though. Yesterday we had an easy climb
up Roan Mountain (the highest in
Tennessee) which is 3' shorter than
Mt. Washington). The trail was lined
with spruce & fir trees which were
big reminders of Maine. Both Maggie
& I loved the smell of them - The
guidebooks say that for North bounders
(Nobos) this is the last time they'll
see spruce & fir trees until New
England.

RAINY

Today as we hiked along we came to an old apple orchard filled of apples on the trees. We picked several which were delicious. This was a "lazy" day. Yesterday was long, although nice, so today we decided to sleep in and just come 8.7 miles to this shelter. We got here about 3:00 so had time for writing, reading, relaxing—even to play a game of cards! With us at this shelter tonight is Navigator, a young man whom we met last night at the shelter. He's personable + fun—and is from Orono, Maine! So, 3 "Mainers" are here at the shelter. At dinner we talked about where in Maine we'd like to be right now + why! He knows many people Maggie knows because he went to Farmington.

It's definitely fall here—leaves are changing + temps are getting colder—40° at night, 60°-70° during the day—perfect hiking weather.
        Love, Reg

Dear Maria,

I have to tell you about the trail names that long-distance and thru-hikers on the AT use instead of their real names. These names are quite unique and are sometimes decided by other hikers, based on something peculiar or unique that has happened to that hiker on the trail. Slughand was named by his dad because he put his hands on a rock to pull himself up and there were several slugs on it; Gistofit was always saying, "I've got the gist of it"; Lemonjello (accent on the second and third syllables) was named because he loved lemon Jell-O . . . other hikers pick their own names because of something they recognize in themselves.

Uncle Marty gave me the name Blueberry because of how much I love to eat blueberries, blueberry muffins, blueberry pancakes, etc. Also, the whole theme in our kitchen in Maine is blueberries. There have been others on the trail with the name Blueberry, but I still use it and answer to it as easily as I do to Peg!

When I hiked with Darcy for the 100-mile wilderness, she picked Sal for her trail name because as a child, she looked like Sal in the book *Blueberries for Sal* by Robert McCloskey. Since I was Blueberry, it was always interesting to us when someone put the two names together and thought of the book!

Trail names are easy to remember and help hikers remain anonymous on the trail. As a hiker, when you sign in at a shelter, you use a trail name—other hikers remember the names because they are associated with particular characteristics of individual hikers. Once after my long-distance hike in 2000, my niece Maggie was at a party at Prescott College in Arizona and met two guys who had been hiking the AT the same summer I was. She told them her aunt had been there and that my trail name was Blueberry. They replied, "Oh, we know Blueberry. We met her in Massachusetts for the first time." When Maggie told me that she had met Nomad and Crest, I knew immediately who they were.

Speaking of Maggie, when we hiked together from Virginia to Georgia, we talked extensively about what her trail name should be, but nothing seemed to be just right for her. Her college major had been peace studies, and she is a Quaker, so we thought of Peacewalker and other similar names, but she couldn't decide . . . Anyway, she usually signed in for us at the shelters as just Blueberry and Friend, and finally, her name really became Friend . . . perfect for her.

Funny thing, isn't it? These names! In my other life/the nonhiking life, if I get a phone call or e-mail for Blueberry, I know it's from a hiking friend.

I've made a list of several of the trail names and will share these with you sometime.

Aunt Peg/AKA Blueberry

Trail Names

These are just a few of the trail names I remember from my hikes:

Blueberry (Me!)
Friend
Sweet Patooty
Tooty
Niko
English Stu
Sal
Carolina Creepers
Grizzly
Eagle Eye
Iris
Jackrabbit
Dirty Bird
Skinny
Wooley Bear
Nomad
Crest
Mighty Dog
Gistofit
Music Man
Golden Boy
Elderberry
Mother Goose
Father Time
Lemonjello
Forbin and Mabel
Trail Shy

Roady
Slipknot
Fancy Feet
Peter Pan
Tinkerbell
Federal Express
Lady Leaper
Shadow
Mushroom
Orion The MOB
Bombidil
Texas Red
Wholesome
Red Top
Gypsy
Drop Off
Sideshow
Dreamer
TinMan
Slughand
Mikey

WHAT ARE THE DANGERS ON THE TRAIL?

Dear Maggie,   7/2000
    This is an amazing trip—
I'm loving it and all is going
well— Remember those scary
things your friend told you about
the AT? None of that has
happened to me! The trail
community is very supportive,
friendly, helpful—

It's never absolutely safe to do anything and wouldn't it be a humdrum
affair if it were . . .

Dear Maria,

Re: Dangers on the trail!

Running out of food, becoming ill, and hurting myself are some of the dangers I think about as I plan for a hike and actually do the hike.

Luckily, I've not experienced any of those in the years I've been hiking. I do take precautions, though, and I thought I'd pass those onto you—although I'm sure you are aware of how to take care of yourself out there.

I very carefully plan my food and water and always carry an extra meal in case of an emergency with food; also, I carry more water than necessary (and as you know, water is a heavy item!) so that if I get to a shelter or tenting spot which doesn't have water, I'll have enough.

As I plan for any hike, I find out all I can about the terrain, water sources, possible resupply places so that there are no big surprises for me when I actually do the hike. This is in such contrast to my early (in my twenties) camping/hiking trips when Uncle Marty and I would just throw stuff in the car and take off! I remember hiking from Chincoteague Island to Assateague Island in sandals, carrying a seventeen-pound tent, a jug of gin and lemonade, no water, no sunscreen in ninety-five-degree temps! While that worked for a fun adventure, these days I am much more careful!

I layer my clothing and am obsessive about keeping an extra shirt and a fleece in a dry bag in the middle of my pack where moisture can't reach it. If I am caught in a downpour and find myself wet and cold when I stop hiking, I immediately shed my wet clothes for the dry ones hidden deep in my pack. Once on a hike with Brigid and Laurie, we had two full days of rain and cold weather. We finally stopped at a shelter to regroup, make some tea, and get warm. Laurie and I switched to dry clothes, but Brigid did not; she continued to wear a wet shirt and layered dry clothing over it. As we sat in the shelter talking, suddenly she said, "I'm dangerously cold!" Her cue for that was that our talk started to be garbled, making no sense to her. Immediately, we got her into a sleeping bag, had her change out of the wet shirt, filled our water bottles with hot water, put those in her bag, and made her drink hot tea. In about two hours she was back to herself, but it was a good lesson for all of us.

Recently, I have discovered that the hand warmers and foot warmers which you can buy very cheaply and which I've always used when skiing are great to have for those cold, rainy times hiking as well. Another item which I'm now including regularly in my food bag is a package of Jell-O. For those really cold moments when your energy is low, hot Jell-O is great—the combination of warm liquid, the sugar, and the protein in the Jell-O is a boost to your body.

I'll write more about dangers later . . .

♡ aunt Peg

Dear Maria,

More about dangers on the trail . . . .

I am fortunate to have been able to avoid getting sick on the trail. Certainly, though, there are plenty of opportunities for hikers to get sick . . . it could be a cold, the flu, some sort of infection or perhaps giardia from a water supply . . . In order to keep myself healthy on the trail, I continue the routine I have in my other life, i.e., plenty of exercise (not a problem on the trail!), plenty of healthy food, plenty of water, and plenty of sleep. Because hot water to wash your hands is not always available, I carry a small bottle of Purell (before that was available, it was a small bottle of bleach!) to use after using the outhouse and before eating. The potential for being dirty is great when you're hiking, as you well know, and washing up before bed or in the morning does not take on the same thorough procedure we use at home. I've found that hikers handle this in different ways. Some don't wash at all and the dirt and sweat become a part of who they are on the trail. Others find a routine that works for them. I use my bandana and wet it to wash my face every evening. If there is a stream nearby, I like to soak my feet and wash the dirt off my legs. If there is no stream, the dirt may just stay there until I do find a stream for washing.

While I know you must know this next piece of advice, I am compelled to mention it any way! If you use camper's soap, even biodegradable, it is not proper to wash with it in the stream. I take a pot of water, put the soap in it and move to a place twenty-five feet or so away from the stream to wash, and then dump the water.

I am horrified to think that years ago we used to actually wash our dishes in the streams . . . yes, that was in the Dark Ages (my early twenties!) . . . Thank goodness, I have become much more aware of taking care of the environment. Occasionally, I still see day hikers who are unaware of how they contribute to water or land pollution. I actually find myself picking up after them or gently suggesting that they wash their dishes away from the stream.

Well . . . that's all for now . . .

You may think that I'm not cautious enough on the trail, but I think you'd be pleased to know that I am very careful — even today I took a side trail which was to be used in the event of in-clement weather — It was threatening rain so I decided that was the best choice, although I really wanted to climb over the rocks & cliff!

excerpt from a letter to Mom —

Dear Maria,

Re: Dangers on the trail; How do you keep from getting lost in the woods?

An important question as I am obsessed with being sure that I don't get lost! I religiously follow the white blazes on the trees! If I start somewhere in the middle of the trail, I use the information in the guidebook to locate the trailhead. It will be marked and there is an indication of south/north, along with the white blazes on the trees in both directions. The trail itself is usually visible as a well-worn path; however, when in doubt, look for a white blaze on a tree. If I go ten minutes without seeing a white mark, I stop and retrace my steps until I find a white blaze. There are places, particularly in a state park or forest where there are many other trails, and it's easy to get off track if you don't pay attention.

The shelters are marked often with a sign or sometimes with a blue blaze (side trail). To keep from coming out of a shelter or camping spot in the morning and not knowing whether to go right or left (north or south), either make a note to yourself as you go off the trail or put something like an arrow in the dirt to show which way you'll head in the morning. When you are tired at night, it's easy to forget which way you turned!

Fortunately, I have never been lost for any length of time . . . I am comforted by the sight of a white blaze and am ever vigilant as to where I am on the trail.

♡ aunt Peg

Dear Maria,

Re: Are you ever afraid on the trail?

As I mentioned to you, that is the number one question I get asked by almost everyone! Even though I usually think they are really asking, "Aren't you afraid of someone doing harm to you on the trail?" I respond, "Afraid of what?" and then I go on to say, "No, I am not afraid of being attacked by a bear or bitten by a snake or killed by another human being or getting sick or hurting myself by falling . . ." I simply am not afraid of those things in either my hiking life or my other life. I love the quiet of the night in the woods with the sounds of animals nearby; I enjoy meeting all sorts of people on the trail and have never felt uncomfortable with anyone I have met. I sometimes tell those who ask if I'm afraid of the male hikers, "No," then I say that I think the fact that I look like everyone's mom or teacher really works to my advantage! Other hikers are always friendly, interested, and supportive/encouraging in their interactions with me. Age and experience really are not factors separating individuals on the trail. We are all out there because we love the hike, the challenges, the culture of the woods . . . those who don't hike do not understand that and are the ones who ask if I carry a handgun or another weapon to protect me from whatever I'm supposed to be afraid of! The answer to that question, by the way, is a resounding, "NO!"

Love,
Aunt Peg

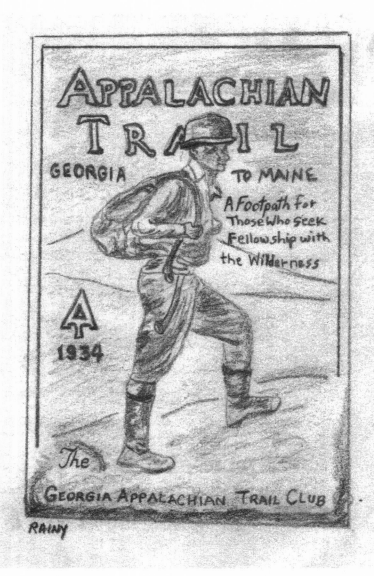

Where Do I Sleep?

Martha + Dave, 7/2000
　　Here's a good laugh for you! Yesterday I had just started hiking from the Inn at Long Trail + I was going through a picnic area when a man stopped me to ask where I was headed – Anyway, he was surprised + called his kids over to say, "Look kids, here's a real backpacker! She's slept outside for 25 nights!" They all said, "WOW!"
　　I had a good chuckle about that –
　　　　♡ Peg

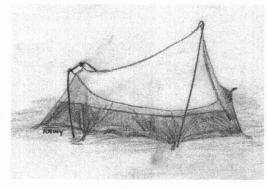

Dear Maria,

Re: Where do you sleep?

I love to sleep in my tent! It's very light weight to carry and easy to set up. Once I am in it with all my gear, it'd be hard to fit another person even though it is advertised as a two—to three-person tent. A few times when my niece Maggie/Friend and I were hiking, we both slept in it, but the quarters were pretty snug, I usually put my backpack in the end opposite the door and use that as a pillow, sleeping with my feet at the door. There are inside pockets on the side of my tent so I have places for my headlight, glasses, and other small items.

I often choose to set up my tent near a shelter because there is a water source and usually a privy there, along with other hikers. The social scene is nice after a long day of hiking alone. Frequently, I do decide to stay in the shelter, particularly when I know the others who are there. On the trip from Virginia to Georgia, Maggie and I met a number of hikers who became good friends. We would travel separately during the day, sometimes meeting along the way for lunch—and then meet at the shelter for the night. Since we hiked in the fall, ending in November, the shelters were warmer at night than our tents, probably because of body heat! We also would use the tents for additional coverings over our sleeping bags if we were in the shelter.

I wrote an article for the paper about sleeping in shelters when I came back from the hike in 2004. It was never published, but I'll include a copy of that here because it tells all about sleeping in the shelters.

Love,
Aunt Peg

The Luxury of Wooden Platforms

After hiking on the Appalachian Trail for two months this fall, I returned to the comfort of my queen-sized bed piled high with a down comforter, quilts, and several pillows. The first morning I arose from that luxurious bed, I discovered a stiff back and some sore muscles! "How could that be?" I asked myself. I had just hiked 700 miles, carrying forty to fifty pounds in my backpack and slept for fifty nights on the hard wooden platforms of the AT shelters—without an ache or pain. "Our bodies are designed to be out there hiking," was my niece/hiking partner's answer . . . and perhaps that is so.

My travel vacation this year was not your typical vacation for a fifty-seven-year-old woman—there were no relaxing airplane rides, cruises, or train trips with hotels to accommodate my every need. Instead, a series of shelters, three-sided structures with an open front and a wooden platform for sleeping, formed the chain of "hotels" I would stay in and grow to appreciate much more than the luxury of a four-star hotel.

The shelters are positioned about every ten to twelve miles along the 2,100-mile trail which stretches from Springer Mountain in Georgia to Mt. Katahdin in Maine. The 700 miles I covered this trip took me from Virginia all the way to the end of the trail at Springer Mountain. Although the shelters are very simple in design, each has its own style and personality. Typically, they are located near a water source and often have a privy somewhere nearby. The size designates the number of people that a shelter can accommodate, ranging from six to twenty-four. It's community sleeping with all the typical sleeping issues, e.g., the snorers, the talkers, the middle-of-the night bathroom breaks, etc. Then there are the issues of sleeping which are not necessarily common, e.g., mice running over your head or sleeping bags in the night, potential visits from bears or other animals, and the possibilities of snakes or spiders resting where you are resting. In spite of all that, the shelters have a magical attraction for hikers and are a welcome sight after a long day of hiking.

When one first arrives at a shelter, the common practice is to read the journal; it's a little like registering in at a hotel. A journal is left in every shelter as a way for hikers to check in, leave messages, and make comments about the shelter or trail. Information passed via the journal might be: "Watch out for the rattlesnake that lives by the tree near the spring" or "A big black bear appeared here at dusk last night."

After checking the journal, a spot is claimed in the shelter, gear is put down, and sleeping bags are arranged. Then each hiker has a typical routine at the shelter. Water gathering, food preparation, and journal writing are the usual activities, but, also, it's a time to exchange conversation with fellow hikers.

The conversation usually relates to what the hike that day was like, the weather, animals or plants seen; seldom does it center on life outside the hike/trail. Occasionally, though, the conversation around a fire at night might become philosophical with reflections on what impact the hike has had on people's lives.

My memories of the many nights in shelters this fall continue to be very vivid and alive even though I now am living back inside my snug, warm house with my husband and cat . . . views of woods and trees that you can see just before you go to sleep and immediately upon waking, laughing with others while playing Farkle (a dice game) on the wooden platform with everyone wearing a headlamp, eating oatmeal in our sleeping bags on cold mornings, reading *Charlotte's Web* in my sleeping bag and then passing it to others who want to read it, everyone taking a rock to bed in case of a bear visit in the night, sharing food and creating a shelter buffet, celebrating Halloween with costumes and treats from our food bags, and being surprised by a hiker who went extra miles in order to get to the shelter where we were . . .

It may not be a vacation that everyone wants to take and for that I am grateful. It was, however, a life-changing vacation for me, and, in the words of a fellow hiker, "We are not the same as we were before we started"—a fitting tribute to an incredible vacation.

Peggy Stout
Finksburg, Maryland
December 2004

Dear Maria,

Re: Hostels and huts!

Besides sleeping in my tent or at a shelter along the trail, I sometimes sleep in hiker hostels or huts.

The hiker hostels along the AT and the Hut system in the White Mountains are great places to stop for a night's respite from your tent or the shelters. I have always taken advantage of those and have planned my trips with those overnight stops in mind.

Each hostel has its own personality and charm; they are places I'd never even known about and most of them aren't available to car tourist/day hikers. It's all a part of that hiking life . . . camaraderie with others who are on a similar path as you, who appreciate the outdoors, and, who are for the time committed to a simple life. The hostels cater to that—simple bunk beds, well used comfy furniture, opportunities for community conversations, meals, and support.

The huts are a bit more upscale, yet still retain a rustic, simple ambience. Because they also cater to day/weekend hikers, reservations are a must and two giant meals (breakfast and dinner) are included in the price which is significantly higher than the typical $10 price of many of the hostels. Many hikers, however, work to stay in the huts . . . a good system for the hiker and the hut.

I have included many letters about both the hostels and the huts to give you a personalized view of these unique halfway house connections between the hiking world and the other world! Also, you will find details of both the hostels and huts in the guide books and AT companion book.

♡ aunt Peg

Dear Suz,   10/3/04

    We've had an incredible day of
hiking - the weather was beautiful
+ we climbed up to our first
"bald" - a grassy top mountain
with a panorama view - we
had lunch next to a waterfalls
which was lovely - and now we
are staying in a shelter which
is an old barn converted to a
shelter. We are on the lower
level (It's huge + could sleep 30
upstairs) which has one side
open - We face the east + a
beautiful view of mountains,
valleys, trees + a field full of
wildflowers. We should be able
to see a great sunrise tomorrow
AM.

-2-

    Yesterday we stayed at Kincora - a
hiker's hostel - which was great -
showers, laundry, an upstairs bunk
room, a kitchen with stove, refrigerator, sink, plus - wonderful people who
own it - a retired couple from Vermont.
By the way, we are in Tennessee now!
    Anyway, we got in around 4 - shower-
ed, washed clothes - then ordered a
pizza with another hiker. All together
there were 5 of us staying here, including a 67 year old woman from
CA. The people who own the hostel
told us to "eat up" whatever was in
the refrigerator so this AM Maggie +
I made breakfast for everyone - pancakes,
scrambled eggs, hash browns, sliced
tomatoes - a hiker's feast!
        Will close for now -
            ♡ Peg

10/8/04

Dear Marty,

Well, here we are back on the trail after the night in Erwin, Tennessee at Miss Janet's Hiker Hostel! What an experience that was! It felt like I was in one of Anne Tyler's novels – a great short story could be written about any of the towns or hostels we've stayed in – especially this one – Erwin is a small town of about 5000 – the main street looks like a typical main street in any small Maine town. When we got near to where the trail came out onto a road, we stopped at the campground to get our package + Navigator (who has been hiking with us for a few days) called Miss Janet's for a ride. She sent another hiker who happened to be there – "Mountain Dew" to pick us up. She or someone at the house is always available to take hikers anywhere! The house is a medium sized house in a neighborhood just off Main St. (nice because we could walk to the PO, restaurants, etc. in spite of the fact that Mountain Dew was there to be our own personal chauffeur! Miss Janet is probably in her early 40's – very friendly, generous, fun-loving, talkative – has 3 daughters – one in college, one 18, one 15 who live there. The hostel is basically the whole first floor of the house – front

– 2 –

porch, nice big living room with TV, VCR, etc. — two hiker bunk rooms...3 bunks in the one we stayed in + 2 in the other, 2 bathrooms and a big kitchen, plus a large yard out back. Everything on the first floor is available to the hikers — there's even a hiker refrigerator. Anyone can cook, use the sink, use the computer, use the washer + dryer (she actually will wash your clothes for you if she's there + is doing laundry!). People are everywhere! Yesterday Miss Janet had to be gone most of the afternoon with her daughter so when the phone rang, Maggie answered it, took messages + even arranged a shuttle pick up for one of the hikers! People just sort of take over + do what needs to be done. While I was doing laundry, I washed all the dishes in the sink — Another hiker emptied all the garbage cans — another swept the floor. There were about 10 people (hikers) staying here last night — great trail camraderie — off the trail!

Maybe we should run a hostel?!! I think it'd be fun — well, must close for now — Lots of love, Peg

July, 2000

Dear Deb + Rick,

Well, I'm having an amazing time on this trip! The hiking has been great, although very challenging at times. It seems like I climb 2-3 mountains every day. Today was a perfect day of hiking - an easy 10 miles up a lovely mountain with great views & then down through spruce, fir, pine trees and a "pine sidewalk."

I sleep mostly in my tent which I really love - it's very cozy, warm, and comfortable. I also, though, have slept in many co-ed bunk houses (the Huts in the White Mountains & hostels), as well as some of the lean-to shelters. I've gotten very used to sleeping in a bunk room surrounded by young, very smelly men (not that I'm much cleaner!). Usually the small towns right on the AT have hostels & for $10.00 or so you can get a bunk with sheets + a blanket and a SHOWER!! These are places I'd probably never get to experience in my "other life."

Take care - I'll write more later -
♡ Peg

July 26, 2000

Dear Amy + Jim,

Hello from my tent in the Maine woods!

This hiking trip has been really amazing — I've loved every minute of it, although sometimes it has been pretty challenging! The hardest parts have been in NH — The White Mountains with a 25 mile trek across the tops of the Presidential Range — and then the Mahoosuc Range in Southern Maine. There is nothing, though, that I can't do, no matter how tough it seems & how sore my knees feel!!

I've had the opportunity to stay in some unusual places — places that I might not normally choose, but that I'm enjoying — Many towns near the AT have hiker hostels — $10.00 a night for a bunk (you do have to sleep in a room with many others) — I've stayed in a retreat house + a "tent cabin", as well!

♡ Peggy

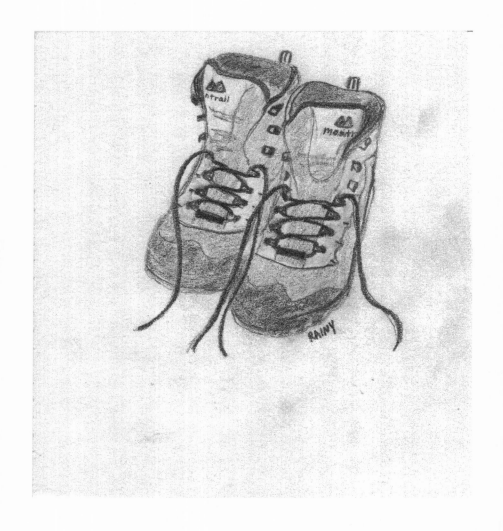

WHAT DO I EAT?

Typical Hiking Day Menu

Breakfast: Oatmeal, tang, tea, possibly a hard boiled egg

Mid-Morning Snack: A granola bar or hiker's bar* or
breakfast cookie*

Lunch: Peanut butter & jam on a mini bagel, a piece of
fresh or dried fruit, a piece of cheese

Afternoon Snack: Gorp* or power bar or hard boiled egg

Dinner: Hydrated ground beef mixed with mashed
potatoes, fruit, hot chocolate or chocolate bar

*Recipe included

As it happened before, we are not able to carry all we can eat - it's called the "Green Monster" in your stomach & most hikers have it after a few weeks - uncontrollable hunger! When we get to a hiker hostel or a town, we go crazy eating everything!

Dear Maria,

Re: Food: What do you eat?
How much food do you carry?
How do you resupply?

Well, I must say right upfront: Food on the AT (or any of my hikes) is extremely important! As I hike, I find myself thinking about food a good portion of the time . . . what will I have for lunch and dinner are constant thoughts. I don't think it's possible for me to carry all the food I need so I tend to be regimented in my planning, what I carry, and how I eat. I can carry food for five to six days and then need to resupply. Food is heavy so that determines what I carry and eat. I like variety, I like fresh fruit, and I like a balance! Interestingly, I tend to run out of enthusiasm for certain foods so what worked for one long-distance hike may not necessarily work for another. I have gone through my love for tootsie rolls, pop tarts, flavored oatmeal, M&Ms, lunar bars, and prepackaged meals, so now I tend to put together combinations that I enjoy in my nonhiking life!

Some of the staples of all my trips include:

- Peanut butter and raspberry jam which I mix together in a small plastic container.

- Hard-boiled eggs . . . here's a hiking tip for you: you can keep hard-boiled eggs up to twelve days without refrigeration if the shells don't break. I usually carry four, having learned that carrying seven or eight is difficult because they are heavy! I eat these eggs plain or mix them with a small packet of mayonnaise (Uncle Marty is very diligent about collecting those packets from restaurants for me!) to make egg salad—one of my favorite lunches.

- Tuna in a package . . . this is a new packaging invention which I love . . . easy to carry, lightweight, and the right portion for lunch or dinner. I mix a couple of mayonnaise packets right into the package and then put it on a bagel or tortilla for a scrumptious meal. The chicken in a package is also good and I often have that with rice for a dinner.

- Kiwi . . . a small fruit which isn't as heavy as an apple but is very satisfying for the fresh fruit craving.

- Dehydrated ground beef which I make myself. I package 1/4 lb. in small Ziploc bags. At lunch time when I know that is what I want for dinner, I put the ground beef into my plastic jar along with water to hydrate the beef. By the time I stop for the day, the beef is soft and ready to be heated up with mashed potatoes for a tasty dinner.

- I seldom buy the dehydrated foods which come in packages at the outfitter stores. I did start out with those but found that they tend to be expensive, full of salt, and the portions are usually too much for a single person. That being said, however, many of my hiking friends use these all the time and love them! I tend, however, to like shopping for products I need, repackaging them into combinations and portions that I like.

- Hiking long distances requires extensive planning for the food and how to resupply. As I plan a trip, I always read the guide books so I know where the towns are and what is available for a grocery store to resupply. Also, I prepare packages ahead of time with supplies, addressing them to post offices along the way. Uncle Marty keeps track of where I am and sends me the packages when he knows I need them. Sometimes he or friends come to meet me and, of course, they always bring supplies then.

- I must say that the day of hiking after a resupply is always challenging as there is extra weight. The trick, of course, is to eat the heavy stuff first to lighten the pack . . . so you can see, there are many things I think about when hiking that are not ever thought about in my other life!

♡ aunt Peg

Mom,   6/2000

My appetite is huge! Once I got my "trail legs", I also got my "trail appetite." You'd love to see all the guys eat – they clean up anything that's left, eating it right out of your bowl if you offer it. Early on I had some left overs and always offered them to others. They were most appreciative! These days I eat every shred of my food!

Everyone is cooking their dinners now + its fun to see what they are fixing. The music teacher is a gourmet, and has a whole supply of spices! Another time I'll plan my food more creatively—
♡ Peg

June 29, 2000

Dear Suz,

Got your package + letter today - right on schedule in Stratton Mtn. Village (Vermont) - Thank you!! I had an interesting adventure getting to it. Yesterday about 5 I arrived at the top of Stratton Mtn. (where you can't camp), so I told a couple of guys, who were there working on a bird study, my dilemma + they said, "Oh, just sleep tonight in the Eco-Center (a tent-like science center structure) + tomorrow the gondola will be working on test runs + it'll take you down to the village - So, I did sleep there amongst the science artifacts + this morning I rode down the gondola with some machinery they were sending down - I got my package from you + one from Marty, had breakfast at a café (by the way, you'd laugh at how I am eating - I think, "Now, what's the least likely thing I'd order to eat," then I order it! Today it was scrambled eggs, bacon, cheese on a croissant, juice, coffee, 2 donuts!) ... so you see, my appetite has increased and I'm into eating fat.

There was a supply store there + I bought a rain cover for my pack - then

-2-

went to the "Village Provisions" store — bought cheese + 4 little bottles of wine. I got a ride back up the mountain on a 4-wheeler, re-packed my backpack (which, of course, is heavy with all the new goodies) and hiked only 4 miles to this shelter which is lovely + new — I decided to stay here as it was pouring down rain. It's newly built — sleeps 20+ because there are 10 built-in bunks + a loft, plus a porch. I decided to sleep in a bunk instead of setting up my tent in the rain. The shelter is all open in the front so I hope the bugs aren't bad — if they are, I'll burn one of those bug sticks you sent me!

Anyway, as I write this, I'm sipping on the wine (well worth the weight), eating cheese + pita bread — what a life!!

 Peg

RAINY

Doug & Linda,   September, 2004

Damascus was fun — Marty & I
stayed at the Lazy Fox B+B — Maggie at
a hiker hostel. The breakfast at the
B+B was amazing — I thought you'd
appreciate the menu:

- Ham
- Bacon
- Sausage
- Biscuits & gravy
- Blueberry muffins
- Fresh fruit (mango, kiwi, strawberries, pears, bananas

- Scrambled eggs
- Grits + cheese
- Home fries
- Baked apples

- Peach cobbler with whipped cream
- pancakes

- Freshly squeezed OJ
- Wonderful coffee

All this was on the table & served
family style — I ate some of everything!
you'd have loved it, Doug!
♡ Peg

10/14/04

Dear Mom & Mary,

Thanks so much for the letters and care packages! We are loving the cookies (everyone else is also). We have spent the day getting the re-supplies all organized, washing clothes, etc. Tonight we ate dinner here at the hostel. The guy who owns the hostel (Elmer) is a gourmet vegetarian chef so for dinner he made: broccoli soup with coconut milk & cilantro, salad (huge & beautifully arranged) with tahini dressing, an African layered dish — couscous with vegetable stew, feta cheese & roasted almonds, and apple pie with ice cream. It was delicious!

We head out tomorrow (Friday).

Love,
Peg

7/10/00

Dear Mart,

I think I'll write a continuing commentary for the next few days as I travel in the White Mountains; "the whites" are really fun and, of course, challenging! Thank goodness for all the climbing Maggie, Barb & I have done in Baxter— I am well equipped to handle these rocks & mountains, but it's slow going! This AM I left the hut at 8:00 — just arrived at this hut at 3:15, going about 7 miles — Some people aren't even here yet & they left when I did. The first 3 hours were incredible — On top of Mt. Lafayette it must have been blowing 50 mph with visability at 10-20 feet. I was very grateful that I had my pack on because it crossed my mind that the wind was strong enough to blow me over!! Don't worry — I've survived that & by the time you get this, I'll be out of the mountains. I was also very grateful for your jacket — it was perfect over my long sleeve blue shirt — I was warm & dry —

-2-

The food at the huts is great. Dinner last night was: tomato bisque, Greek salad, homemade garlic bread, steamed veggies, rice, dijon chicken and chocolate cake — all yummy + as much as you want to eat! Breakfast this AM was cream of wheat with cinnamon, brown sugar, granola, + pineapple for toppings, grape juice, coffee, pancakes + sausage. There are college kids working here — they are friendly + funny - In the AM (6:30) they wake everyone up by playing songs on the guitar, ...

Tuesday: 7/11/06 - Here I am at Zealand Falls Hut - a beautiful hike today after an ominous weather report this AM. Skies cleared about 10:30 + it was gorgeous, except for the wind on top of the mountains: 40-50 mph! I wore your jacket again all day which was nice — Stopped for lunch at a spot where I could see all these mountains up close.

I can smell bread baking in the hut - I think I'll soak my feet in the falls while I wait for dinner.

This is all for now - Love, Peg

June 12, 2000

Dear Mom,

This is day 3 and all is going well! I spent the morning in a lean-to with 3 others because it was raining so hard. Finally it stopped and I packed up & headed for the next campground where I am now. The hike was beautiful - I kept walking through tunnels of mountain laurel all in bloom. The campsite tonight is in an area with tall pine trees - very pretty. There is the funniest "privy" here - I followed the sign & there it was - no building, just a toilet seat on a box over a hole! I'm going back in the AM to get a picture!!

RAINY

My "food" has been good — tonight I had the "spinach cheese omelet" (a prepackaged meal). It ended up more like scrambled eggs but it was good & more than I could eat. Last night I had lasagna, the first night turkey tetrazzini. Breakfast is tang, oatmeal, and coffee. Lunch is usually peanut butter & jam on a bagel or tortilla or cheese on a bagel. Today I had lentil couscous soup because I was still at the shelter. I have much more food than I need so will leave some with Suz when I see her.

I'll close for now — I'm writing this by flashlight which is not easy —

Love, Peg

- Day 7
- 14 + miles
- On top of a
  beautiful hill-
  camping
- Sunny & breezy

Sept. 15, 2004

Dear Suz,

    All is well — Tonight Maggie & I are camping on top of a beautiful hill/field/meadow covered with wild flowers and surrounded by mountains. We passed by an apple tree just down from here and we each had a wonderful apple from it. This is the first night we haven't stayed in a shelter but it's 5 miles from here to the next one and when we arrived at 4:00 we decided this was it! Maggie has been wanting to sleep under the stars (she's been in shelters each night) so she will here.

I'll sleep in my tent, as usual, but am leaving my rain tarp off as there's a great breeze and it looks to be a starry night.

As soon as I finish this letter, we'll start dinner. For me, it'll be pasta with pesto. I'm sure it'll be tasty — I use angel hair pasta because that cooks quickly & I'll put an envelope of dried pesto + a little bit of olive oil right into the pot as I cook the pasta — then we'll eat out of the pot! As you know I only have one pot & even though I do have a bowl, it seems silly to dirty the bowl, especially when water for washing the bowl & pot is at a premium! — Some different from the way I operate at home, huh?!!

Last night I had roasted garlic mashed potatoes with ground beef that I had dehydrated — Beans & rice the night before + Mackenzie's Chowder (potatoes, navy beans, veggies) before that.

Meals are odd – just one dish usually. I don't have a huge appetite yet and am not "loving" my snack or lunch choices. I have had 10 hard boiled eggs with me which is good, although 10 is too many to carry! They're heavy – next time will only bring 4 or 5. I've made egg salad twice which was yummy! This morning I had 2 eggs chopped up with olive oil & parmesan cheese – a very tasty combo! I also have brought tuna in a package container (not can) & it's great.

Yesterday we rounded a corner on the trail and discovered a cooler filled with sodas & cookies – "Trail Magic" from Super Dave – a nice treat.

Tomorrow we'll arrive in Pearisburg – We're looking forward to pizza, salad, beer, showers, the phone and mail!

Love, Peg   10/2004

RAINY

105

Dear Maria,

I thought you might like these recipes . . . both the cookies and the bars are sources of high energy and many calories. I make them often for my hiking trips as they keep well in my pack and are perfect snacks for those moments when you desperately need some sustenance!

Enjoy!

Recipes for Good Hiking Food

Hiker Bars—from Brigid Demand and Laurie Philips

- 3 cups oatmeal
- ½ cup peanut butter and ½ cup melted butter mixed together
- ¾ cup brown sugar
- ¾ cup honey
- ½ cup raisins
- ½ cup finely chopped pecans

Spray Pam on a 9×9 glass pan. Mix all ingredients and spread into pan. Microwave for four minutes. Cut into wedges or squares. These are great energy bars!

Breakfast Cookies
Nona & Fot Thompson

Cream the following:

½ cup butter
2/3 cup brown sugar
1 egg
1 cup vegetable oil
1 teaspoon vanilla extract

Add the following in the order shown:

1 cup toasted rolled oats
1 cup Grape-Nuts cereal
½ cup peanut butter
2 ½ cups white flour

1 teaspoon baking soda
1 teaspoon salt
1/3 cup + 1 tablespoon toasted wheat germ
1/3 cup + 1 tablespoon oat bran
1/3 cup + 1 tablespoon nonfat dry milk powder
1 cup raisins
1 cup toasted chopped walnuts

Form into 1-inch balls. Place on ungreased cookie sheets. Bake twelve to fifteen minutes at 350 degrees. This recipe makes five dozen cookies.

Keeping Food Safe on the Trail

Every shelter in Shenandoah and some in the Smoky Mountains have bear poles for hikers to use to string up their food. It's not easy to do if your food bag is heavy. There's a long hook and you put your bag on the end; then lift it up and hook it over one of the hooks. It's about fifteen feet tall, so it takes a lot of strength.

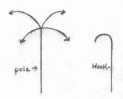

Many times there are no bear poles, so the food bag has to be tied up in a tree . . . the process for that is not easy for me! You have to:

- Find a tree with a sturdy branch ten to fifteen feet off the ground
- Throw a rope up and over the branch, usually with a rock tied to one end of the rope for weight. This is the tricky part as it often takes several tries to get the rope over the branch.
- Then, tie the bag onto the rope and pulley it up.
- Finally, tie the other end of the rope around the trunk of the tree.

It's quite a process, but one I don't neglect. I never keep food in my tent as I don't want to attract any night visitors.

In some areas, New York and New Jersey particularly, there are bear-proof canisters near each shelter, so hikers can put their food bags there at night. I love it when I find those . . . they are easy to use and I don't have to look for a tree to string up the food bag.

WHAT IS DAY-TO-DAY LIFE LIKE ON THE TRAIL?

8/8/2000

Dear Bob & Sally,

I'm having a wonderful hike + am actually in the last leg of this trip — 10 days in the 100 mile wilderness right before I climb Mt. Katahden in Maine (the northern end of the AT).

Today was a perfect hiking day — We did 12.5 miles through a lot of spruce + fir trees — past many beautiful streams + two spectacular waterfalls. We sat on a granite ledge for a break, ate blueberries that were growing there + watched some birds eating red berries off a big bush. We startled a ring necked pheasant — swam in a stream under a waterfall + even washed our shirts! What a life! ♡ Peg

Hiking takes commitment, perseverance, goal orientation, and flexibility—plus inner strength and determination . . .

Dear Maria,

As you know, I have used letter writing to family and friends as a way of daily chronicling about all my hikes. Also, in my other life, I end each day by writing in my gratitude journal five things that I am grateful and I continued to do that whenever I was hiking . . . so, not only do I have tons of letters which people returned to me after each hike, but I have those gratitude entries. Here are some selected entries from my hike in 2004 which I thought would give you a sense of the highlights of each day.,

Love,
Aunt Peg

GRATITUDE JOURNAL ENTRIES

- 9/9/04
  - Marty's love + support
  - My energy
  - Maggie's easy "way"
  - Muscle memory
  - A spectacular part of the AT

- 9/11/04
  - Finally arriving at the shelter
  - Friendly folks at the shelter
  - Maggie's stamina
  - Great rocks, beautiful views
  - Being able to sit way up on Dragon's Tooth

GRATITUDE JOURNAL ENTRIES

- 9/13/04
  - Seeing a bear
  - Beautiful fields & wild-flowers
  - Good conversation with Maggie
  - Varying terrain
  - Laurel Creek Shelter

- 9/14/04
  - Day 6!
  - Ferns, rocks, trees
  - Another day of good weather
  - Finding someone to get a message to Marty
  - Mashed potatoes!

GRATITUDE JOURNAL ENTRIES

- 9/15/04
  - Camping high up on a mountain
  - A lovely breeze
  - Seeing the sunset
  - Feeling peaceful
  - Interesting food
- 9/22/04
  - Rows of rhododendrons
  - Morning sun through the trees
  - Fording + not falling in the stream
  - A message in the shelter book from Pisses in the Wind
  - Time to be in the moment
- 9/24/04
  - An easy beginning to the day
  - Finding a place to camp
  - Panoramic scenery
  - Anticipating the Dairy Queen
  - Having hiked 15 days

June 11, 2000

Dear Sug,

Day 2 has been eventful! 4 of my personal hiking nightmares have occurred today, but I'm happy to report that all have been handled successfully! This AM I came to Guiness Brook, a beautiful spot with a raging river/ brook that I had to ford — that means taking off my boots, socks, putting on my river sandals + walking through rough (knee to thigh high) water with my back pack on. Luckily, Barb + Maggie + I had experience with that a couple of years ago in Maine so I knew the tricks!

Nightmare #2 — I was way up on a

-2-

mountain + suddenly with no warning a huge thunderstorm with wind + driving rain appeared. I managed to get my poncho out + covered myself and the backpack. It rained hard for 15 minutes + everything was soaked. Luckily I had dry clothes in the middle of my pack so I changed right there.

#3 In an effort to avoid taking off my back pack I decided to try to pee standing up, pushing my shorts + underwear to one side — You guessed it! I peed all over myself!! Luckily, I'm travelling alone + not long after that the rain came + totally soaked everything —

#4 I had to walk across 2 log bridges (it's like a balance

-3-

beam which I've always had major problems with). I made it across, though, "without incident," ie. falling in!!

Right now I'm in my tent & it's pouring rain — Luckily, I got the tent up before the rain started — If it doesn't leak tonight, it'll never leak!

Must close — ♡ Peg

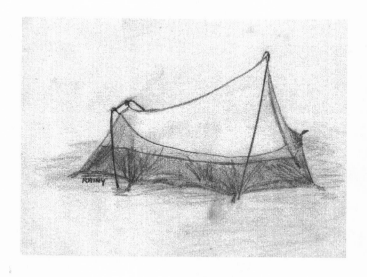

Dear Jean + Shahid,   10/29/04
    We thought we should let you know
that we had a very exciting evening of
farkle* games last night! Thanks so much
for the game + instructions. My friend
Laurie is here with us now, hiking for
6 days — it's great to have her fresh
enthusiasm + energy with us. Last
night she, Maggie, Niko, + 2 other hikers —
(Goose Dreams + Deaf Balance), + I were all
in a shelter together so we decided to
play Farkle — it was great fun + very
loud, as you can imagine!! Actually,
you'd have loved the whole evening
because the talk turned to what
everyone was going to do when finished
with the trail — One guy is going to
propose to his girlfriend and has
already picked out the ring — We had a
great discussion about marriage,
how you know the person is right,
etc. I threw in a lot of the questions
we put together for the marriage
book + some of the "wisdom" we had
collected. It was really interesting
as everyone was very vocal about

116

-2-

marriage, relationships, etc. → Then we moved into responding to the "latest" question, "What have you learned out here?" I think I've learned to totally trust the universe — things always work out here... anyway, good conversation + farkle games made it a great night!

We really appreciated you coming to Hot Springs, bringing our supplies, treating us to dinner, etc.! As always, everyone loved you guys + several times you've been mentioned!

The Smoky Mountains were great + now we are looking at under 100 miles to go + 8 days. It's hard to believe. Goose's comment last night was: "We'll never be the same as we were before we started... we can't really go back." I think you realized this to an extent... it's much more than a hiking trip in the woods — The whole experience of hiking, meeting other hikers, solving problems, having time to reflect + dream + plan has been incredible

Well, must close for now — Thanks again for everything.
Love, Peg

Dear Suz,   10/23/04

It's Saturday, but I know I'll pass by a mailbox tomorrow so I thought I'd write to you today— We're in the Smoky Mountains — in a shelter tonight with 9 people — last night there were 15 people — way too many! It caused me to feel very irritated about the "weekend" hiker — loud, obnoxious, not concerned about "Leave No Trace," etc. Anyway, as I was hiking this morning, I spent time thinking about the NEGATIVES of hiking long distances — I decided you'd be a good one to vent to:

#1 — Being dirty all the time with no good way to wash.

#2 — My hair — of course my roots are dark & white in places &

—2—

don't wash it for a few days, oks terrible!

#3 — I don't wear deodorant nor do I shave my legs

#4 The shelters are often dirty & you sleep on wooden platforms, sometimes next to people you don't know.

#5 — In the shelters there are often mice who run over your head in the night — or get into your pack — or both!

#6 — You have to hang your food on big bear cables in the trees & if it rains the rain goes right into the food bag —

-3-

#7- Throughout Tennessee + in the Smoky Mtns, there are often no privies/toilets so you have to take a shovel + go to a designated "toilet area" - totally NOT pleasant!

#8 - There's no place to "dry" your clothes this time of year other than in the bottom of your sleeping bag - so, often in the morning, you put on a cold, damp sports bra + shirt (you only have one to begin with).

" So there you go - the list of negatives which just become part of what you do every day!

Hope all is well - Take care.
♡ Peg

RAINY

EXCERPTS FROM LETTERS

This morning I left a 6:30 to get an early start on Killington — it turned out to be a great hike, up, over + down! Going up was like going up through a narrow tunnel of fir trees, rocks + roots — It was raining a little and very misty so it kind of felt like going through a movie set — Not real life!!

♡ Peg

7/2000

June 21st (summer solstice) is "Hike Naked" Day! The 6 guys who stayed where I did last night all hiked naked today — apparently they were quite a hit as they crossed the AT bridge over the Mass. turnpike!

6/2000

Dear Mary,   July 22, 2000

I thought you would most appreciate this AT experience! Tonight I am camped on the banks of the Kennebec River near Caratunk, Me. It is very peaceful, quiet, beautiful. Suddenly, there are many ambulance, fire engine sounds - close by - so I go to see what is happening + discover that there has been a bad car accident down the road and a helicopter is coming to land in the field directly in front of where I am camping - there are many people directing things, fire engine + an ambulance here - lights, etc. + after about 30 minutes, in it comes!! What excitement!! Marty had dropped me off about 5:30 + I had said, "Oh, I'll just read a while + go to bed early" not knowing all this would consume my attention!!

Dear Jill,   6/2000

You asked what the first part of the hike was like — Well, my first 2 nights I had dreams about work — which seemed so out of place here — but I guess it was "unfinished" business! Now I don't remember my dreams + I am sleeping long hours (9–6??!) My main concerns are: how many mountains/hills will I climb today, what will I have for dinner, what should I get rid of to make my pack lighter! It's amazing to go from one life to another — kind of puts things in perspective when you get overloaded at work or with the annoying details in life, like laundry, etc.

More later — Peggy

Dear Mark,   6/2000

The one thing I did not plan for in this 2 month hike was how to deal with how much I miss you! All the time I wish you were here to share this experience. Truthfully, for at least the first week I'd get up in the AM, come out of my tent, and say to myself, "What am I doing here?!" It is an amazing marriage we have — me being able to go off for this 2 month adventure by myself + you being so supportive + encouraging of it — Life is certainly good!

Lots of love, P.

123

Dear Tom & Kitty,   10/16/04

    It was great to get your letter when I came into Hot Springs — This hike is really incredible — I feel very fortunate to be able to spend two months out here — hiking, climbing, camping — just being outside. I love having my niece Maggie as a hiking partner. Her trail name is Friend so we are known as Blueberry & Friend. We've only met one other woman hiking any distance (she is 67 years old!) — all others are men — mostly in their late 20's — there are a few retirees.

    Tonight it is very cold (40's) — we have a big campfire going & 5 of us are here at the shelter.

    The mountains in Tennessee & NC. are really spectacular — There are many day hikers out on weekends; it seems as though the folks in this area really use the trails —

        More later — ♡ Peggy

Dear Suz,   July, 2001
    I am writing from the AT so
please save this & send it back!
    Darcy & I started yesterday on a 3
day hike to climb the Bigelow Mtns (in
Maine) — We didn't get started until
5 or so — hiked an hour & pitched our
tents on the side of the Trail — that's called
"Stealth" camping — It rained all
night & again today — I would describe
this day as "Rainy & Challenging." We're
hiking about 30 miles in 3 days — late
this afternoon we pushed on (instead of
stopping at 4:00) to climb West Peak, a very
steep, difficult climb — we were tired &
it rained torrents making the rocks
slippery — plus the wind blew fiercely
when we got to the top! We're now in
our tents, having set up in the rain —
we cooked a quick dinner & are
exhausted. Once I finish this, I'll be
asleep in one second! ♡ Peg

Monday, 9/16/02

Dear Jeff,

I hope all is well with you. I think of you all the time. This section of the AT is very nice - pretty & not too many mountains. The only unfortunate thing is that both yesterday & today I got caught in terrible rain. It was not a surprise yesterday as I started in rain, but today was sunny & hot & then suddenly, a downpour! It was about a mile to this shelter where I am now so I hurried along and when I got here I was soaked. This is a very nice shelter - It's large, has bunk beds (no mattresses, of course) and a big porch with room for many people to sit. Also, there is a separate place with a picnic table & a cover over that - Then it has a "shower" - an outdoor one with water from a spring. No one else is here & now the sun is out so I am sitting on the porch drinking hot chocolate with brandy & eating gouda cheese - it's quite nice! I have all my stuff spread out so it'll dry - last night it rained very hard - my tent did not leak, but I had to pack it up wet this morning.

Today has been the day of the butterfly - dark blue ones have been everywhere - I'm keeping my eye out for snakes because many people have seen them - none for me so far at least.

126

Dear Suz,   July 25, 2003
This was a perfect hiking day! No rain, nice breezes, beautiful views — we slept in, then made breakfast on a tent platform which overlooked the mountains we climbed yesterday — Our climbs today were steep, but early in the day. Tonight we are staying at Cranberry Stream Campsites — We've set up our tents & put all our stuff out to dry. The stream is beautiful — lots of rushing, cold water. We soaked our feet + generally washed up some. Today we saw many cave like structures in the big rocks which were spectacular. The only bad thing about being here are mosquitoes which are unrelenting in their search for places to bite. I've moved into the tent to finish this so I can escape being bitten!

June 27, 2000

Dear Tara,

Greetings from the AT somewhere in the Vermont woods! Today was an interesting day for hiking — for 4 hours this morning I hiked in a torrential downpour. During that time I contemplated the top 10, then reduced to the top 5 reasons a person should hike in the pouring down rain! So here goes —

#5 – you hike faster because you take no breaks!

#4 – You get to wear your rain gear + see if it works!

#3 – there is definitely a mystical quality to the woods when it rains!

#2 – there are no bugs biting you!

#1 – you know you're a "real" hiker because the "wanna be's" would Not be out in the rain!

-2-

My first 10 days were pretty limited to seeing just the thru-hikers who started in March. Now that school is out for most people, it seems that they have hit the trail. There is still a lot of solitude in the woods and often a whole morning goes by before I see anyone on the trail.

Connecticut was rocky & mountainous; Mass. was flat, rocky, swampy & muddy and now Vermont seems like a long, green tunnel! The woods everywhere are beautiful — green & lush.

How lucky am I to be able to do this?!!!

♡ Peg

Bear Mountain Inn

4/29/2010

Dear VJ + Tony,

Greetings from the AT! You
Probably know that I am hiking the
AT in New York + New Jersey (162
miles altogether) which will finish the
whole 2100 miles of the AT.

I was thinking about you guys
today + thought I'd drop you a line.
Today was not what is a normal
hiking day on the AT! — So, this is
how it went: I woke up in the
shelter I stayed in last night — that
was odd because it was the picnic
pavillion on the ball field of a monastery
in New York! The ball field was adorned
by many statues of Jesus + many
crosses. Still, it

PO Box 351, Bear Mountain, New York 10911
845.786.2731 | fax 845.786.2543 | visitbearmountain.com

is nice that the friars (let's remember to ask Aunt Barbara what the difference is between friars, monks + priests!). Open this shelter to hikers as the AT goes right through their property. So, I ate oatmeal + peanut butter on a bagel + headed out — Within 15 minutes the trail crossed a road + there was a Shell station with a Jiffy mart! I went in + indulged in a great cup of coffee + a donut. Then I hiked on — the woods in New York are beautiful + the hiking is pretty easy — about noontime I came to a side trail which I took to a place called Anthony's Nose (that's what started me thinking about you guys!). Anthony's Nose is an outcrop of rocks overlooking the Hudson River. The views were great + it was very high up, but I couldn't see anything that looked like a nose! (I did read later that no one is sure how that name was

Bear Mountain Inn

given). So then I continued hiking for another hour until I came to a big highway with lots of traffic + a bridge — the Bear Mountain Bridge — which the trail crossed. It was very high + about as big as the Bucksport Bridge in Maine — it crosses the Hudson as I was walking across the wind was very strong + practically blew me over. I'm not afraid of heights, but I didn't particularly care for that bridge walk. Then the trail turned into Bear Mtn. State Park, going straight through a zoo! (Hikers don't have to pay!). It was a great zoo with all the typical animals + exhibits. After the zoo the trail

PO Box 351, Bear Mountain, New York 10911
845.786.2731 | fax 845.786.2543 | visitbearmountain.com

continued on around a lake & right up to the Bear Mountain Inn where I am staying tonight — not in my tent or a shelter but a fancy Inn with the Bear/Moose theme. I just had a pizza delivered & will eat that & head to bed early as tomorrow will be a day of total woods hiking, no diversions like today.

The weather so far has been rainy & cold & windy — even snow flurries the other night. Today it was sunny, but still chilly. Typically, I wear all my clothes to bed to stay warm: 3 prs. pants, 1 long sleeved shirt, 2 fleeces + some times my jacket, 2 prs. socks, gloves + a hat. That usually keeps me warm in my sleeping bag. I do love being outside all the time — for 2 days this week I didn't see another person — I miss the conversation but I like the solitude. Well, this is all for now — Please save this letter & give it back to me for my book. Thanks — Love, Aunt Peg

June 16, 2000

Dear Mart,

It's hard to believe that this is Day 7 on the trail! The sun is out today so its been great hiking (70's, not 100's). I'm in Mass. now & tonight I'm at a new shelter which is going to be "dedicated" tomorrow AM so the Ridge Runner is here for the night. I think I'll stay in the shelter instead of my tent because it is rather impressive for a lean-to. It has 4 bunk bed platforms (no mattresses - ha!) and a loft. It would probably sleep 10-15 people.

I have been taking lots of pictures as the scenery & views are really spectacular. I feel like I am walking through a Sierra Club calendar!

In Conn. there were many stonewalls, beautiful ravines, and incredible brooks, streams, and waterfalls. So far in Mass., there have been steep, rocky places for miles on end and some mucky places. Every day I go up and down a mountain. So far they are not bad, but I know that'll change when I get into Vermont. I feel like I am following a trail of Mountain Laurel — they are just blooming here and are beautiful.

More later — ♡ Peg

RAINY

GRATITUDE JOURNAL ENTRIES

- 9/29/04
  - an easy 10 miles out of Damascus
  - The Hiker's Breakfast at the Lazy Fox
  - Trail camaraderie
  - Friends at the shelter
  - Good conversation, a big bonfire, and a full moon

- 9/30/04
  - An amazing day to hike
  - 16+ miles unexpectedly
  - Finding our strength
  - Maggie's healed foot
  - The beauty of the sun through the trees

- 10/04/04
  - The climb up Roan Mountain
  - Fir + spruce trees on the trail
  - Taking it leisurely
  - Company + good conversation at the shelter
  - Being at the shelter with another "Mainer".

GRATITUDE JOURNAL ENTRIES

•10/06/04
- Trail Maintenance; men
- An easy day of hiking
- Lunch on top of Beauty Spot
- An incredible setting for a shelter
- Sharing dinners

•10/11/04
- AT companions
- The magic bucket
- My tent
- Being able to hike in the fall
- Feeling fit

•10/12/04
- The unexpected cliff walk
- Trail magic - apple pie
- Anticipating Hot Springs
- The challenge of the hills
- Interesting conversations

GRATITUDE JOURNAL ENTRIES

- 10/14/04
  - Jean & Shahid's thoughtfulness & generosity
  - Learning to play Farkle in the bar
  - Mail from so many people
  - The Sunny bank Inn
  - Clean clothes, showers, & re-supply

- 10/18/04
  - The Universe providing!
  - The 40th day
  - The first night in the Smokies
  - Stu's fire building skills
  - A fire, music, good food

- 10/22/04
  - An early AM start
  - Cooking breakfast at Clingman's Dome
  - The beauty of the Smokies
  - The depth + scope of this experience
  - The coziness of my sleeping bag

EXCERPTS FROM LETTERS

I am very dirty tonight—layers of sweat, mud, skin-so-soft, + aloe on my muscles make an odd combination of smells...Two young men stopped here for a snack a while ago + then headed into "town"—They said they hadn't had a shower since New Jersey!

I do wish there was a way to do this hike + have a shower each night, but I think I remember as kids we only had a bath once a week — good preparation for this!!

Interestingly when I meet a day hiker on the trail, I can smell their laundry detergent — their clothes are so clean!

I am very dirty and I smell — and I'm getting used to it - all the hikers smell bad!!

EXCERPTS FROM LETTERS

One bit of excitement on the trail today was that 2 Boy Scouts had been with a big group and had gotten lost — so separated from the group. The as we headed up a trail Search & Rescue people asked us to keep an eye out for the boys — about 2 miles in, we found them — stumbling down the trail!

Maggie is doing math facts in her head & speaking Spanish in her head as she hikes up the long, arduous, steep ascents — Martha will be happy to know that!

EXCERPTS FROM LETTERS

The hiking in this part of VA is easier than I had anticipated — The trail is beautiful, lots of very tall, old trees, some pastureland, and some orchards. Yesterday I went by several apricot trees - most of the apricots were on the ground smashed or half eaten by animals, but it was nice to think about when some farmer must have planted those trees.

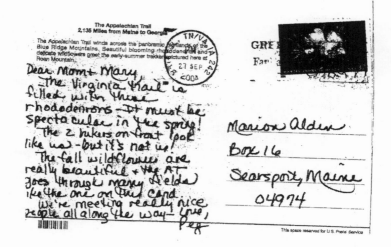

Dear Mom + Mary —
The "Virginia Trail" is filled with these rhododenrons — It must be spectacular in the spring!
The 2 hikers on front look like us — but it's not us!
The fall wildflowers are really beautiful + the AT goes through many fields like the one on this card.
We're meeting really nice people all along the way — Love,
Peg

Marion Alden
Box 16
Searsport, Maine
04974

Sept. 13, 2004

Dear Mart,

I hope all is well — I'll be glad to talk to you when we get to Pearisburg — which is going to be a day later than expected. This section is tough with many mountains & our 3rd day of 13+ miles up & over two major mountains about did us in — we didn't arrive at the shelter until 7:40 that night... so we revised a bit & are taking an extra day. We will try to find someone tomorrow to call you & tell you so you won't worry.

I always forget how hard it is in hot, humid weather carrying heavy back packs!

♡ Peg

RAINY

Today I am in a beautiful spot, high up on a ridge & staying near a Shelter — there is No water, unfortunately, but someone has left a gallon jug half full — a nice surprise — I anticipated no water because of a note in the last shelter log, so with what I brought & this jug, I have plenty.

EXCERPTS FROM LETTERS

You asked if I were reading on the trail – yes – I have "thin" books – Classics & mostly children's Classics. "Thin" means Not heavy in my backpack! When I finish a book, I leave it in a shelter for someone else to read – The most popular, by far, has been Charlotte's Web – It takes on new meaning when you read it as an adult! Several other hikers requested to read it when I finished!

On this trip I've read: The Red Tent, Black Elk Speaks, Beauty, The Good Husband, Jewel, and now a Joseph Campbell book. I read before I go to bed every night in my tent – the same ritual I have in my "other" life!

EXCERPTS FROM LETTERS

Mt. Washington is known for having "the worst weather in the world" — subject to change at any minute.. that's just what happened today. It was sunny with bright blue skies and suddenly a thunderstorm came up. I was hiking along with 5 others + we were doused with cold rain, loud claps of thunder and close hits of lightning...we hurried a long for the last 3 miles to the hut where I'm staying tonight — There was no place to get under cover so we just schooched down + moved from one rock to another —

RAINY

June 15, 2000

Dear Mary,

Today has been a perfect hike! Yesterday I totally re-arranged my backpack, sent a bunch of things home and washed/dried wet clothes at a laundramit — hence, I reduced the weight by 8 lbs. and what a difference! I had breakfast in Salisbury with some other hikers and then headed out. It's the first day I haven't felt totally wiped out by noon. I think my body has finally decided that this is serious business and I'm not going to stop, so it's responding to the challenge! Everyone tells me that the first two weeks are the hardest and that I need to go slowly so I've definitely amended/discarded that lovely left-brained "itinerary" I created and gave to practically everyone!!

RAINY

Thanks so much for sending me the skin-so-soft bug/tick repellant/sunscreen. I have it on right now as a matter of fact & no bugs are biting! ♡ Peg

Day 53   11/1/04
Walasi yi shelter
70°

Dear Blake + Katie,
        Greetings from Georgia! We're about
40 miles from Springer - it's been an
amazing trip + I can't believe we're now
into the last few days. I have loved having
Maggie as a hiking partner. I loved being
alone the first hike in 2000, but this time
it's been great fun + much more social with
her along. We've met many other hikers -
Maggie, of course, is a magnet for all the
young male hikers in their 20's - and I, as
her aunt, am always popular! We have met
very few women hikers, though. For the past
2 weeks we've been hiking with a guy from
Long Island, Niko, and a guy from England,
English Stu - that has been fun. Also, my
friend Laurie from Chicago left today after
joining us for a week.... So the evenings in
the shelters have been great. We've been playing a dice game called Farkle which is
hilarious + easy for everyone to learn.
        Hiking in the fall is really wonderful -
we have had mostly great weather - during the
hurricanes, we coincidently happened to be
in towns - we spent the Ivan hurricane

-2-

in Pearisburg, Va. We've had only 4-5 days of hiking in the rain + luckily — no snow.

This southern section seems to be much "easier" than the New England section, although there are plenty of mountains to climb with long steep ascents. The Smoky Mountains were definitely a highlight of this trip, although the shelters were always very crowded!

As you know, by now our appetites are out of control! We think + talk about food all the time — the food in our food bags seems very boring! I can hardly wait for an apple pie with macintosh apples.

The whole hike is much more than just walking the trail — I'm sure you remember that from your days on the trail — We feel very fortunate to be able to do this.

Take care — looking forward to chatting with you about all this when I'm back in the "other world"! ♡ Peg

RAINY

Sept., 2009

Dear VI & Tony,

I thought of you on this recent section hike of the AT. We were in the Maine woods where there were many places we had to "ford," that means "to cross a river or stream." The water was high this year because of all the rain we had this summer. One river had a rope across it — from one tree to another. The water was up to our knees so as we crossed we held onto the rope so we wouldn't fall — the rocks were very slippery & of course we had our backpacks on & our boots around our necks! You'd probably have loved it!!

I was happy to get to the other side in one piece & no falling!!

♡ Aunt Peg

* When doing a water crossing, be sure to unfasten the waist belt to your backpack in case you should fall!

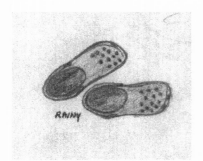

Some people have sandals to wear when crossing water — I have a pair of "crocs" which are great. They dry easily, are very lightweight & are an extra pair of shoes to wear when I take my boots off....

June 23, 2000

Dear Doug + Linda,

Greetings from the top of Mt. Greylock in Mass. This is the highest point in Mass., but is hardly high by Maine standards! It was a beautiful day to walk up + tonight the sunset is incredible. I'm actually staying at the lodge on top of the mountain — it's right on the trail + not much of a splurge since they have hiker rates ($22) — I had a shower + a great dinner!

This has been an incredible trip so far — I'm enjoying the total time outdoors + the challenge of everything. I do have some blisters, Linda, but am handling them better than 18 years ago! I do still remember the trick of aspirin in the AM to dull the pain!!

I think of you guys often as I am loving my walking stick — everyone comments on it!

The first week I struggled to do 7-8 miles a day but finally I have my trail legs + did 18 the other day — the most so far.

I thought of you, Doug, last week as it was 90° + I was road-walking past a really swampy section — I passed by an Irish pub + went in + ordered a "triple thick milkshake"!! They were a little surprised, but they made me a great one.

149

July 4, 2000

Dear Martha, Dave, Z, M, A,

What a trip! All is well – my appetite is huge, I've already increased the size of my feet & ankles – Apparently, this is common for long distance hikers (sometimes your shoe size changes a couple of sizes!), and I am finally able to do 12-15 miles a day easily.

Tonight I'm camping near a shelter with some hikers I met over the 4th at the Inn at Long Trail in Killington – That place was a real treat! Showers, laundry, beds, an Irish Pub, telephones – all the amenities! Plus, one hiker's wife came with a ton of food & a huge box of homemade cookies.

I've met some great people & we become fast friends in a short period of time –

Tomorrow Marty is meeting me in So. Pompret, VT in the afternoon. He'll stay the weekend so I'll take a "Zero Day" on Saturday. I'm looking forward to seeing him, needless to say –

Will close for now – Love, Peg

July 3, 2000

Dear Mom,
Tonight I'm staying at a shelter just south of Killington. It was raining when I got here about 2:00 so I decided not to do the last 5 miles up. It was a good decision because it has been raining ever since, but is supposed to clear tomorrow. I set up my tent right in the shelter as it's large with an overhanging porch. There are 7 of us here + a dog! — a mother, daughter couple from Waterville, Maine, a music teacher + his dog, a couple of teachers from CA, a woman who is 68, + me! The conversation is interesting — right now they are discussing the fact that your feet get permanently longer after you have hiked a long distance — we'll have to see about that —

-2-

Today 4 of us had breakfast together at a little restaurant just .3 of a mile off the trail — it was called the Whistle Stop — I had French toast that was outstanding. I had them make me a turkey "grinder" which I took with me for lunch + then again for dinner tonight —

As I was hiking along today I came to a stream which had cans of coke in it — a "Trail Nome" leaves them there for hikers, 5 of us sat on the bank, drank cokes + ate lunch.

I'm not sure I told you about the "Cookie Lady". — Her house is .2 mile from the trail + you can stop there for cookies + water. She keeps them in the freezer + puts them in the microwave for a minute or so — they tasted like they were fresh from the oven! Yum — That's all for now. P.

September 9, 2004
Day 1

Dear Mom + Mary,
Well - we're here! - and the first day was great. The torrential rains that were predicted did not occur - The weather was sunny with blue skies all day. Marty dropped us off at 8:30 at the trailhead - We hiked 9.5 miles - got to the shelter about 3:10 which was good time for the first day. The trail today covered 2 mountains + a beautiful ridge walk. We saw 4 deer + a skunk. The shelter tonight is deep in the woods + no others are here, there's a great stream down in front so we were able to soak our feet & clean up when we got here. Maggie is a great hiking partner - We go at about the same pace + have the same ideas about how to do things. Wherever we go together we get lots of attention - because of her!!

My pack weighs about 45 lbs. and hers a bit more - 50 lbs. probably. When we first weighed our food bags, hers was 18 lb. + mine 9.5 lb. We had a good laugh about that! She took some things out to

152

reduce the weight. Marty will meet us in Damascus Va. on the 28th - so then we will decide what we need to get rid of - he's also bringing lots of things we didn't take in case we want them.

We're having him send boxes of resupply items (food) to Pearisburg, Va. + Atkins, Va. - and then some other places, as well.

Tonight for dinner Maggie had beans + rice + cheese + tortillas; I had spaghetti with red pepper pesto sauce, a kiwi + dried fruit. We both had chocolate after dinner.

While we may have some sore muscles neither of us has blisters tonight! I think my muscles have "memory" of hiking so it didn't seem as hard today as it did the first few days last time.

Tomorrow we have only 8.5 miles, but two large mountains to go over. This area is surrounded by mountains which are beautiful.

Marty got me a small, extremely light weight radio with earphones so I have it on now - which is nice - the weather for the next 5 days is sunny + clear according to the radio report!

Well - it's about 8:30 - I'm in my tent as it is very dark already - I think Maggie is asleep already? So - I'll close! Please be sure to write to her as she's afraid she won't get any mail!

I'll write more another time.

Love,

Peg

July 21, 2000

Dear Tom & Kitty,

Thanks for your cards at my mail drops – I think of you guys often & of our Katahdin trips.

I'm having an incredible time on this trip. Yesterday, though, was the most challenging physical activity I've ever done – the Mahoosic Notch in southern Maine. It's described as the "most difficult mile" of the AT and, indeed, it was! It took me 3 hours to get through it. It's the bottom of a canyon between 2 mountains. The canyon is filled with house sized boulders which you have to climb over, under, around or through caves to move along. There was snow in some of the caves & some deep holes with cold streams running through – All in all, it tested every muscle I had! When that was done, I had to climb straight up over rocks, roots & slick rock for another mile. Luckily, I camped at the top of that on Speck Pond – a beautiful spot –

My new mantra: "If I can do Mahoosic Notch, I can do anything!"

More later –

♡ Peggy AKA Blueberry –

Mahoosuc Notch

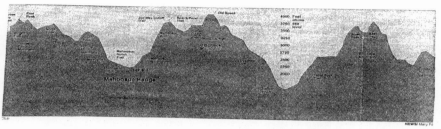

Day 32   10/11/04
Jerry Cabin Shelter
-Sunny

Dear Jeff,
Right now I'm in my tent which is
very cozy - it seems like it'll be cold
tonight - The shelter is small + dingy -
potential for mice so I decided to set
up my tent! Maggie + two others are in
the shelter. We hiked 14 miles today -
3 miles straight up - a pain, but the day
was nice and we covered lots of
different terrain. There was some
"trail magic" at one point - a white
bucket, hanging from a tree, filled with
granola bars, applesauce, cans of mixed
fruit - We helped ourselves + left a
note.
        I think about you all the time -
Many of the people we meet are about
your age - out here to figure out,
what they are going to do with their
lives - It's a good time + good place
to think about things.
        So far we've been very lucky with the
weather - it's been just about perfect.

-2-

—This past week it was fall-like-sunny, but low humidity. The first week it was really hot. When it rained (the hurricane) we were in Pearisburg in a motel. The adventures have been fun—everyone we meet is interested in who we are & what we are doing.

All our equipment seems to be working well—I don't love my new little pellet stove, but it does work—just takes too long to get started. I may resort to my old stove which is heavier, but more reliable.

There is a guy out here who is carrying his Martin guitar, along with the rest of his gear—apparently he plays for $$ + food. He's just ahead of us (we read about him in the shelter journals!)—We hope to catch up to him soon—just to hear what he plays

The Virginia woods have been beautiful, the terrain is varied—lots of tree topped mountains, valleys + fields. The other night we stayed at a shelter on top of Garden Mtn. It was an open field with panoramic views. We watched a gorgeous sunset as we drank hot chocolate + brandy!

Must close— Lots of love, Mom xxoo

Dear Jean + Shahid,   9/11/04

Greetings from the AT! We're out here — enjoying the experience, although I always conveniently "forget" the hard parts of this! They are! being so sweaty + dirty all the time — We do try to wash off in creeks + streams (No soap, of course), but everything still is smelly — also, at the beginning the ascents which come several x's a day up mountains are very challenging when you have a 45 lb. pack on! As soon as we descend or walk along a ridge top, we forget about the difficulty getting up there! We have already climbed several mountains in the Appalachian range. Today we did Sawtooth Ridge which looks like this from down below: ᴧᴧᴧ - many up's + down's - after that we climbed, Cove Mtn. to Dragon's Tooth, a huge piece of stone like this: ᴧ. Near the top we had to scramble over rocks, pulling ourselves + packs up on iron rings. It was definitely worth it once we got there.

-2-

We are exhausted tonight because the hiking took so long and we didn't get to the shelter until 7:30 — almost dark. When we did get there, there were 2 men hikers from NC — probably in their 50's. They had a fire going so we relaxed a bit, made a quick dinner & now I'm in my tent. As soon as I finish this, I'll be going to sleep!!

Maggie is a great hiking partner — we are similar in many ways so are doing well together. I was telling her about playing Farkle & we decided we'd like to play after dinner some so I was wondering if you could put together a set for me — light weight dice & the rules, points, etc. Thanks!

Must close for now — It is clearly time to sleep! Love,

Peg

July 23, 2000

Dear Joe + Chris,

I was so pleased to get your letters & to hear what you've been doing — Sounds like a fun summer!!

I am having a great hike on the AT — already it's my 43rd day — I'm in Maine now and it's getting close to the last leg of the trip. This coming weekend I'll be in Monson, Maine to meet my friend Darcy and on Monday we will start the "100 mile wilderness." There will be no access once we start that. It'll probably take us 9 days to do and then we'll meet Marty, Jeff, my sisters, Darcy's parents and some others who will all climb Mt. Katahdin with us... and that's the end!!

I thought of both of you last week when I was in the Mahoosic Notch (southwestern Maine). The "Notch" is described as "the most difficult mile" on the whole AT — and indeed, I would agree! It took me 3 hours to go one mile because there are house-sized boulders that you have to go up, over, around or through caves (where there is still snow + ice). Probably you guys would just scramble through all that very quickly & think it's fun, but I was very cautious because I didn't want to fall into any of the deep holes that were everywhere! After I got through the notch, then I had to rock climb straight up the "arm" of a mountain for another mile. I was certainly happy to get into my tent that night!

A couple weeks ago I climbed in the White Mountains which was fun. It was steep, but that's the kind of climbing I like to do. The day I climbed Mt. Washington was very clear so I could see for 80 miles — mountains everywhere! As I was approaching Mt. Washington it looked like this:

Mt. Washington with radio towers →

The path through the rocks looked like this

X (me)

It reminded me of the Wizard of Oz — I was following the "yellow brick road" to Oz!!

Today I had to "ford" three big streams — Not my most favorite thing to do because I have to stop + take off my socks + boots — well, I'll close for now — Have fun in DC + England. Love, Peggy

RAINY

Oct. 5, 2004

Dear Jean & Shahid,

Soon we'll be meeting you at Hot Springs so I thought I'd drop you a line — We got to the shelter early today so are having a pleasant afternoon just reading, writing, and talking. We are travelling (hiking) along the Tennessee-North Carolina border - It is beautiful! Yesterday we climbed Roan Mtn. which is 3' shorter than Mt. Washington — It was spectacular, and has huge "gardens" of rhododendrums at the top.

We are having a wonderful time — the hiking is great and we are meeting a number of other hikers — some of whom you'll probably get to meet in Hot Springs — There are very few women — one, though, is Ruth Adams — 67 years old — who has a bad ankle so moves along the trail slowly! Tonight we are at the shelter with Navigator, a young man from Orono, Maine! We met him last night at the shelter + then we hiked here together. →

RAINY

I am intrigued by the fact that most of the young men out here keep journals — not of the day-to-day events, but of their thoughts + feelings — yeah! They write regularly — even stop <u>on</u> the trail to write when they've been thinking through something they want to record. This young man tonight is reading, "As a Man Thinketh" by James Allen — a great book about wisdom, he says!

Maggie + I have created some questions which we ask ourselves + others):
· What do you carry in your pack that is of sentimental value?
· What is the most important thing in your pack + why?
· What 3 things do you miss the most?
Tonight as we were eating dinner, Navigator asked: "Where in Maine would you want to be right now (if you could) + why?" — Lots of good - interesting conversation out here!

I gave Marty the info. about Sunnybank Inn in Hot Springs because it has had rave reviews on the trail — Gourmet vegetarian food + a nice big old B+B. We want to stay 2 nights to re-group.

We've had a <u>dime</u> sighting already! — One day I had been thinking about the dimes + there arrived at the shelter to find a dime right in front of it!

Well — hope all is well with you guys — I'll talk to you before you get this, hopefully — See you soon! Love, Peg

Sept. 26, 2004

-Relax Inn
a "O" day
Sunny, breezy

Dear Jeff,

I was really happy to get your letter when I arrived at the Village Inn, now re-named, The Relax Inn! We arrived yesterday thinking it'd be just a one night stop to re-supply, but Maggie's ankles are in bad shape — pulled muscles and/or tendons so we decided to do a "O" day today so she can ice her ankles & stay off them. Tomorrow I will leave in the AM to hike up Mt. Rogers, the highest mountain in VA. She'll stay here until Dad comes in the afternoon — then they'll meet me at the Mount Rogers Visitor Center + we'll all go on to Damascus for a couple of days. We hope by that time her ankles will be better.

Yesterday we stopped at a shelter before we got to this town + read in the journal that a thru-hiker from last year now lives in this town + if anyone had any problems to call him (Fox is his trailname) — so Maggie called him from here! It turns out that he is an emergency room doctor so he was very knowledgeable about her ankle problems. Today he + his wife (also a doctor!) are going to pick us up + take us to dinner. He'll have a look at her ankles — So, that's some good luck — Trail Magic, they call it! Love, Mom

EXCERPTS FROM LETTERS

.... There have been numerous accounts of "trail magic" out here this time — Last week a sign on a tree near a road crossing invited all southbound hikers to a house nearby for pork barbeque, potato salad, apple pie + ice cream! It was a feast not to be passed up! They even made a big green salad for Maggie when they found out she was a vegetarian — a great couple they were! This whole trail community is an amazing network that no one would know about except for hikers.

P.

10/04

... the other day, in the middle of the woods, we found a ziploc bag attached to a tree — it contained the weather report for that day + the next 3 days! — a fine example of trail magic!!

9/04

Dear Maria,

Farkle is one of our favorite games to play in the late afternoon or evening after a long day of hiking. For it to be really fun there must be at least three people playing. It's a dice game which requires six dice, a level playing space (platform floors in the shelters are perfect), a piece of paper and pen for keeping score, and head lamps for playing after dark.

I've included the directions here for you and am going to send you six dice so you'll have what you need to play the next time you're out on a hike or just having friends over in your apartment.

Often when a group of us plays, our laughter, cheers, moans, and groans which come from either a good roll or a bad one fill the woods, probably shocking the animals that may be lurking about!

Love,
Aunt Peg

A game for two or more players. You will need a score pad and pencil.

OVERVIEW OF THE GAME
POCKET FARKEL is a high-score game in which players roll dice for points. You roll six dice, remove only the dice you want to use for points, then re-roll the remaining dice. Some scoring dice must be removed after every roll. If you can eventually make all six dice count for score, pick them all up and keep going. If none of the dice you roll can count for score, you lose your turn and any points you made during that turn.

OBJECT OF THE GAME
To get scoring dice on every roll, and to be the first player to get more than 10,000 points.

TO GET STARTED
Write all the players' names at the top of a sheet of paper. **Each player must roll at least 500 points during one turn to get into the game.** The player's game-entry score and subsequent scores are added up below their name.

1. The first player rolls six dice and decides which dice they want to use for score. **If they don't roll any ONES, FIVES or other scoring combinations, their turn is over and they must pass the dice.**

SCORING

ONES = 100 pts ea	FIVES = 50 pts ea
SCORING COMBINATIONS	
3 ONES = 300	4 of any kind = 1000
3 TWOS = 200	5 of any kind = 2000
3 THREES = 300	6 of any kind = 3000
3 FOURS = 400	STRAIGHT 1-6 = 1500
3 FIVES = 500	THREE PAIRS = 1500
3 SIXES = 600	TWO TRIPLETS = 2500

2. **Only ONES and FIVES count by themselves.** Other numbers count as three-of-a-kind or more but not in pairs.

3. **Dice can only count for score once.** After dice are removed, you cannot add to them for a bigger score (for example, you can't add a six to three previously-rolled sixes to make four-of-a-kind).

How Many Miles a Day Do I Hike?

> I'm having an incredible trip. Each day it seems like I'm walking through a Sierra Club calendar — the woods are lush & green, filled with beautiful ferns & moss, streams & waterfalls are everywhere. I usually hike 8-9 hours a day & range from 9-15 miles a day, depending upon the terrain.

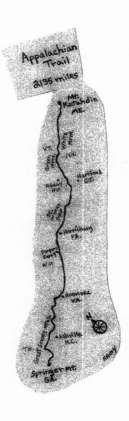

It's a Great Day to Excel (Laurie)

Dear Maria,

Re: How many miles a day do you hike?

    When people ask me that, I usually say that I hike between ten and fifteen miles a day—but it varies due to a number of reasons . . . where I'm headed . . . what the weather is like . . . who I am with . . . how many breaks I take . . . I've been known to hike only five or six miles a day or as far as twenty or twenty-two. Some hikers pride themselves on the number of miles they hike in one day and they even hike in the dark . . . that's not me! I don't like to hike in the dark and I totally subscribe to the theory that each person hikes his/her own hike, setting a pace that works best for any particular day.

    On the hike in 2004 from Virginia to Georgia, I decided to put a weather report and miles hiked that day on each letter I wrote; for the other hikes, I usually kept that information in my gratitude journal. The following are excerpts from the letters.

♡ aunt Peg

EXCERPTS FROM LETTERS

Iron Mtn
Shelter
16.3 miles
sunny —
great hiking

Day 23
16.4 miles
Watuba Lake
Shelter

Day 3
13.4 miles
Sunny +
humid

Day 25
Overmount
Shelter
8.7 miles

Day 30
No Business
Shelter
6 miles from
Erwin, TN
Sunny - 60°

Day 38
Roaring Forks
shelter
11.4 miles

Day 5
Laurel Creek
Shelter
Hot, Sunny
12.3 miles

Day 32
Hogback Shelter
10+ miles

We now have about 250 miles left
(we've gone about 458 miles) to
Springer Mtn. The time is flying!

Day 50
Siler Bald
Shelter
12 miles

The sign in this
lodge says:
582 miles to
Katahdin.
It's hard to imagine
I'll be there by
August 10th!

Dear Maria,

I thought I'd include this potential plan for a hike that Brigid, Laurie, and I did last fall in the 100-mile wilderness (Maine). It gives you an idea of how I determine the daily miles for any hike I do . . .

Love,
Aunt Peg

PS. When we did this hike, we did the first three days as planned—then on day 4 we ended up staying at White House Landing. Then we hired a seaplane to ferry us ahead to Rainbow Stream—we ended on time!

Potential Plan for the AT Hike

9/10: Drive to Greenville/Katahdin Iron Works for AT access—3 to 4 hours from Swan Lake
          Hike 7.3 miles to Sidney Tappan Campsite

9/11:   Hike 9.0 miles to East Branch Lean-To

9/12:   Hike 16 miles to Antlers Campsite; the terrain in mostly downhill and flat.

9/13:   Hike 6.1 miles to White House Landing; take boat to island; resupply; get back onto trail and hike 8 miles to Wadleigh Stream Lean-To; the terrain is mostly flat so it'd be 14 total miles.

9/14:   Hike 12 miles to Rainbow Stream Campsite.

9/15:   Hike 18 miles to Daicey Pond Lean-To; the terrain is flat and very beautiful.

9/16:   Climb Mt. Katahdin; the mileage is 10 miles round trip and will probably take us 9-10 hours; leave park and head back to Swan lake.

********I don't know how to cut the miles per day any more than I have. I have started us at one of the only access points in the 115 mile wilderness because I realized we couldn't do 115 miles in 6 days. The total mileage for this is about 76. As I have indicated, the long days cover very easy, flat terrain. If it looks like we won't be able to do this plan once we get started, we can make adjustments at White House landing via boat or shuttle by the owner. We can look at the maps when you get here and see if you can find any other options. Let me know what you think.

WHAT KINDS OF ANIMALS DO I SEE?

Dear Maria,

Re: What kinds of animals do you see when you hike?

Surprisingly, I don't usually see a ton of animals on any given hike. Collectively, though, I have seen black bears, a moose, a deer, two timber rattlers, a mink, possums, porcupines, foxes, and turtles . . . I have heard but not seen coyotes . . . and then the usual array of birds (including a grouse, a partridge, wild turkeys, hawks, and owls), squirrels, chipmunks, and mice . . . I have no horror stories to tell about encounters with bears, snakes, and moose. I will include a few letters though about experiences others have told me about, as well as a stand-off I did have with a deer and the "snake" dance I did when I heard the rattle of the timber rattler! You'll enjoy those stories!

Love,
Aunt Peg

August 2, 2000

Hello everyone —
    Greetings from the Maine woods! Today was a great day — we climbed 4 mountains by noontime and then, as we were hiking along this afternoon, we saw a bear not far from us! As soon as "he" heard our voices, he turned and ran, but we were quite excited... Yesterday morning we saw a moose when we went to a pond to get water.

Sept. 2002

Dear VJ + Tony,
    While I was hiking on the Appalachian Trail, I saw many black bears! I remembered, VJ, about how you would sing loudly whenever you thought a moose was around when we were in Baxter camping — So I sang loudly when I thought a bear was near! The bears didn't pay any attention to me, though — They just ran when they saw me.
    ♡ Aunt Peg

Sept. 2004

Dear Mant,
    Today was a beautiful day of hiking — We went up + down a mountain, through several open fields.. Saw 2 snakes, a turtle, and a bear! — Also, some donkeys!!!

Shenandoah, 9/2002

Mart,

The deer are very "bold" - they pay no attention to humans and often refuse to move if they are in the middle of the trail and a hiker comes along. Today I had one such encounter! I didn't really want to walk by the deer as the trail was very narrow and the deer was big - I "waited" him out - it took about 30 minutes for him to decide to move. During that time I talked loudly, sang, banged my poles but he stood firmly, staring (glaring?) at me. Finally, he sauntered off — whew! ♡ Peg

June 17, 2000

Dear Mom,

I hiked 15 miles today—the first time I've done that distance so I'm pleased with myself. I'm at a shelter, but in my tent because of bugs + potential visitors, ie. porcupines! The ridge-runner/ranger told about waking up one night in a shelter + feeling something heavy on his chest - he thought he was home + it was his cat, but instead he quickly realized that it was a porcupine!! Needless to say, I'm not taking any chances of that happening to me!

Porcupines tend to gnaw the edges of the shelter floors to get the salt from sweaty legs which have hung over the edge when hikers sit - I now can tell if a shelter has problems with porcupines by the gnaw marks on the shelter floor!!

More later—

Love,
Peg

RAINY

7/26/00

Dear Suz,

Just wanted you to know that many hikers have commented on the pleasant sound of my bell and are interested in the fact that it's an antique sheep's bell. Having a bear bell on my pack seems to be keeping the bears away as I haven't seen any yet!

This has been a great week of hiking — wonderful weather, nice trails (even terrain + fewer roots + rocks), mountains have had gentle slopes + I've passed through miles of spruce + fir trees that smell like Christmas!

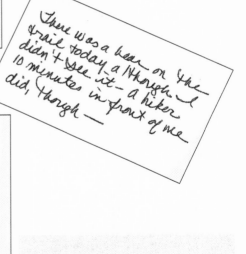

RAINY

There was a bear on the trail today although I didn't see it — a hiker 10 minutes in front of me did, though —

...one of the "tricks" you can use to scare a bear away is to push your backpack up very high on your back so it makes the bear think you are very tall (I guess they don't see well!) — I never had to resort to that as the bears I encountered were way too afraid of me to stick around!

RAINY

4/2008

Well, Mart, I did the snake dance today! Brigid + I were hiking along a lovely stretch — down a mountain, chatting away. Suddenly I heard the RATTLE! (I was in front) — I knew immediately what it was, but couldn't see it! I jumped, leaped + yelled — until Brigid spied it — a very big long Timber Rattler who also hissed at us from the side rock!!

....I got to the shelter fairly early + thought since no one was there, I'd stay in the shelter. After reading the Shelter Journal, I changed my mind! I had noticed that the edges of the shelter floor where hikers sit + dangle their legs were very rough, as if something had gnawed on them. — Right — porcupines in search of salt from our sweat!! Apparently that shelter, for some reason, was a favorite of the porcupines!! — So, I set up my tent + all night long I could hear the porcupines as they came + went — they make a clicking sound as they move!
7/2000

Dear Maria,

Re: Dogs on the trail

I really enjoy the dogs I meet on the trail. Except for the Smoky Mountain National Park and Baxter State Park, dogs are welcomed hikers on the AT. They are usually leashed and well behaved. When I see that a dog is coming toward me, I always ask the owner the dog's name. Calling a dog by his name immediately seems to put him at ease. I do that in my regular life as well.

Some of the dogs I have enjoyed meeting during my hikes are the following:

Mabel, a lovely dog, whose owner, Forbin, was a young man who had just graduated from Virginia Tech and was doing a thru-hike.

Eddie, a brown Dalmatian (not sure of that), that was always shivering; his owner, my friend Brigid, said it was for attention! He slept in a sleeping bag in the tent at night and tried to stay there all the next day; he got a lot of attention from his owner and friend!

Sole was a beautiful white dog that traveled with a couple on a five-day hike. She loved to snuggle with me by the fire at night.

Lester was my friend Laurie's dog, and he hiked with us sometime in Maine. Mistakenly, we left his food in the car, so he enjoyed all the extra foods we carried! He and I became fast friends after a meal of mashed potatoes!

They all wore little packs, usually carrying their own food and the garbage! Your Rita would be right at home out on the trail. I can imagine how cute she'd be with a little backpack!

Love,
Aunt Peg

WHAT DO I HAVE FOR EQUIPMENT?

My titanium pot is working great – everyone who has seen it has commented that they'd like one! I tell them my 82 year, old Mom bought if for my birthday!

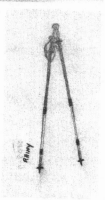

Dear Maria,

Re: What do you take for equipment? What's in your backpack?

Over the years, I've refined what I take in my backpack—mainly to keep down the weight I carry. After several hiking trips, I've figured out what I need and what I can do without. You know, Maria, that in my regular life, as well as my hiking life, I'm a minimalist so it's not hard for me to do without many things; there are, however, some luxuries that I always take such as: a book, paper to write notes and letters, and a small flask of brandy . . .

I'm enclosing a list of clothing and equipment that I made for my friends Jim and Diane when they asked what I carried. The list is pretty standard for all my hikes now.

Love,
Aunt Peg

June 30, 2000

Dear Jim & Di,

Well, today is Day 20 on the AT and all is well — Tonight I'm camped next to a really nice stream so I washed my shirts (both of them), plus had a sponge bath myself. Tomorrow AM I'll wake up early and wash my hair before I take off (I haven't washed my hair in 8 days!). That'll be a treat!

Thanks for your cards. It's great getting mail — sort of like when you were at camp as a kid and mail time arrived! You asked what I was carrying so I thought I'd give you a rundown on that. My backpack holds plenty but I have to be careful to keep the weight down — ideally, 35 lbs. is what I like to carry, but it varies depending upon what I'm carrying for food.

Equipment:
- 1 tent
- sleeping bag
- sleeping pad
- stove
- 1 pot for cooking
- 1 fork
- 1 spoon
- 1 bowl
- 1 mug
- jack knife
- 3 water bottles
- water purifier
- first aid kit
- toothpaste
- toothbrush
- purex
- liquid soap
- maps
- a book for pleasure reading
- stationery for my letters
- headlamp
- candle
- a small flask of brandy
- FOOD!

Clothing: • 1 long sleeve shirt \ these I
• 1 short sleeve shirt / switch
off wear-
ing most of
the time

• 1 pair of zipper off
pants so they are shorts also.
These I wear every day!

• 1 pair of shorts that I wear
into town

• 1 cotton t-shirt that I only
wear at night if it's not raining

• 1 pair of leggings (I wear
these at night or if it's cold
during the day).

• 1 fleece pull over
• 3 pairs of socks
• 3 pairs of underwear
• 1 rain jacket
• 1 bandana
• 1 hat
• gloves, if I think I need
them

June 18, 2000

Dear Jean + Shahid,
     Greetings from Great
Barrington, Mass.! Tonight I
am staying at the East Mtn.
Retreat Center (which is located
.5 miles off the AT) — it is usually
used for large group retreats,
but they welcome AT Hikers if
there is room and there happens
to be plenty of room tonight. The
cost is $10.00 + includes the use of
a great bathroom (and shower) and
the laundry. It is really lovely —
cozy, warm, plus beautiful views.
It has rained hard all day so
I was happy to get here and to
stay the night. I am now clean
of layers of sweat, dirt, bug
repellant etc. — plus, I have clean,
dry clothes.

I walked into Great Barrington &
met friends from Conn. who drove
over to meet me with fresh supplies.
We had a wonderful picnic lunch
in the bandstand in the town
center—as it rained!

This is an incredible adventure—
the first 2-3 days were physically
harder than I anticipated, but
after I lightened my back pack (I
sent a package of things home) and my
muscles adjusted to the fact that
this is what they're going to do
everyday, it's been much easier.

I think about you guys
every day because an essential
piece of my "equipment" is the rain
jacket you gave me! It has rained
6 out of 9 days so far, so I've worn
it often—also, I use it as my
pillow at night. At home I have
always used 2 pillows, but now I'm
well adjusted to my raincoat pillow!!

Dear Maria,

Re: More about equipment!

I am feeling compelled to give you the details of my equipment. I know you are just getting started in your acquisition of equipment, so maybe some of what I tell you will help you figure out what you want. I have purchased most of my equipment at REI (Recreational Equipment Inc.). They know me there and are always helpful, interested in where I am hiking. I suggest that you forge a relationship with an outfitter supply place where you get to know the folks and they get to know you. Personal attention always makes a difference when you are investing in important gear.

Love,
Aunt Peg

My Backpack

I bought my backpack at REI in January of 2000. It is a Gregory (brand name) and is "custom" fit to my body frame. The guys who helped me with it, took two packs apart and created one for me with a woman's small top and a woman's medium waist It fits me perfectly and I have used it for at least 2200 miles!

It has a large compartment for all my gear, a zip-off compartment at the top which I can take off and use for a day hike, side pockets with mesh for my water bottles, zippers to let me enter the main body of the pack from the bottom and front, as well as the top. Straps at the bottom are good for holding my sleeping pad and/or tent on the outside.

The salesman told Uncle Marty I could hike the Himalayas with that pack--- Uncle Marty replied, "Don't give her any ideas!"

Update: In 2009, I got the newer version of this same pack which is much lighter and weighs about 3 lbs. empty as opposed to the 7 lbs. of my other one. It has all the same qualities of the original and I am loving it.

My Waist Pouch

In addition to my back pack, I wear a pouch around my waist. In that I usually put a small package of Kleenex (for toilet paper), my knife, my ID (license), a credit card, and some money. I like to have all these items close at hand for when I need them. When I'm not wearing my glasses, those are there, along with an emergency power bar or some gorp.

I put the map for the day in one of my pockets (in a Ziploc bag).

My Tent

I know I've written a lot about how much I love my tent! Besides the facts that it's cozy, comfortable, and just the right size for me, it's also very light weight (2 lbs) and very compact. Along with it, though, I do carry stakes and a ground cloth (I use a contractor's garbage bag for that).

I have recently purchased a tent hammock which is lighter (1+ lb) with no need for a ground cloth or stakes. I am trying this out as an alternative to my regular tent; it is very comfortable, but I did discover on a recent spring hiking trip that I need a sleeping pad under my sleeping bag as cold air comes up from underneath. It is easy to put up, but, of course, you do need two trees about 12 feet apart for the support. The jury is still out on whether or not this will be a permanent replacement for my tent!

Other hikers use a variety of light weight options. A combination of a tarp and hiking poles is a common option; sometimes hikers have made their own tent using very light weight fabric. Sometimes you will see 3 sided tents with an open front or just netting on the front. Some hikers don't carry tents at all and rely on the shelters or sleeping "under the stars." Besides the obvious weight issue, the decision as to what kind of tent one uses is really based on personal tastes.

Sleeping Pad

Since I usually can sleep well on just about any surface (rocks, roots, etc. don't bother me), I originally didn't take a sleeping pad with me. I discovered, however, that the pad is important because it shields your body from the dampness/moisture on the ground and, actually aids in keeping you warm! Recently, I have also learned that some hikers put the sleeping pad right into their sleeping bag and believe that it works wonders for keeping them warm.

My pad is self-inflating, $\frac{3}{4}$ length---I roll it up and attach it to the outside of my pack. It's good, also, for sitting on outside or in the shelters. I do like equipment which is versatile!

Hiking Poles

When I hiked in the summer of 2000, I used a lovely wooden hiking stick given to me by friends Doug & Linda. It had the carving of a man's face on it. I loved it for the unique carving, but realized that I needed two poles.

Since then I have used a pair of Leki adjustable poles with a triple spring system and cork handles. They have been wonderful---once I adjusted to using them. It's like having another pair of legs to help support you, particularly coming down over rocks, roots, and steep inclines.

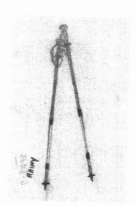

Sleeping Bag

My sleeping bag is a "one pounder" which I purchased in Maine. It does, in fact, weigh one pound! Supposedly it is good to 40 degrees so it's great for spring, summer, and early fall hiking. I did buy a liner for it which is also very light weight and it takes it down another 10 degrees. If it is really cold, I sleep with all my clothes on and I have usually been very warm and comfortable. The bag dries quickly when it gets wet and fits easily in the bottom of my pack.

Cooking Items

For cooking I carry a tiny Whisper Light stove and usually 2 small bottles of propane fuel. One bottle lasts me 3-4 days.

I have one cooking pot---a titanium one which is extremely light. I have one fork, 1 spoon; my cup and eating bowl are made of the new "squish able" material so they are light weight and can be folded up and placed in any small space. Over the years I have sometimes carried a mug with a top for hot beverages and sometimes a plastic plate, but I've decided I don't really need those. What I have is all I need and use!

First Aid Kit

I carry my first aid kit in the top of my pack for easy access. It is small and compact with these items:

- Large and medium sized bandages
- Neosporin (small tube)
- Gauze pads, adhesive tape
- Antiseptic pads
- An ankle wrap
- A needle
- Matches
- Small scissors that fold

Initially, I had many more items in this kit, but over the years I have only ever used these items so that's what I carry.

I do have a small bottle of Ibuprofen which I carry separately.

Water Purification

Whatever you decide to use for water purification is an essential piece of equipment! Purifying water from any stream, river, spring is a must.

At first I used iodine tablets to purify my water. They were very light weight and easy, but you have to wait 20 minutes or so after you add the tablets so you couldn't immediately drink the water. (These days there are many types of tablets or drops which don't require such a wait).

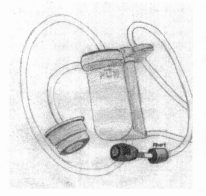

Next I invested in a Pur water purifier where you pumped the water and it was filtered immediately. I liked that better except the purifier added weight and bulk to my pack and at times it was hard to pump the water.

Now I have a steripen which is much smaller, more compact and lighter. It does use batteries but it works quickly and easily So far, I am happy with it. I still, though, carry Sweet drops with me as a back-up!

Personal Care Kit

I have a small personal care kit which I also keep in the top of my backpack. In it, I have:

- Fold-up toothbrush
- Small tube of toothpaste
- Small plastic tube of Ibuprofen & daily meds
- 2 packages of Kleenex
- Small container of purex
- Small bottle of Ben's Bug repellent
- Small hairbrush
- Tiny mirror
- Ziploc bag with 8-10 baby wipes

That's it! Remember, I'm a minimalist!!

Water Containers

I have used Nalgene bottles for a number of years and for a long distance hike, I carried 2 quart bottles and a pint bottles which I strapped to the outside of my pack for easy access.

Now I have a camelback which fits in my backpack with a hose right to my mouth. That is less bulky and easier to pack than the Nalgenes. I do take the pint Nalgene, as well, though.

My Boots

Since I have very long, thin feet and particularly thin heels, finding the right boots was a chore--- I have found them, though, and am on my 3rd pair in 10 years. They are Montrails---a medium priced boot which fits my feet perfectly. I wear my boots all the time...when I hike, of course, but also when I walk, when I work outside, when I need snow boots, etc., so they are well worn in and very comfortable. I wear two pairs of socks: white running socks under regular wool blend hiking socks. All of this, ie. a good fit, regular wear, the socks, keeps my tendencies for blisters under control.

My advice to you about getting a good boot is to talk to others in the outfitter store or other hikers, try on many different types, and go with the boot that feels comfortable. Some hikers like low tops and very light weight hiking shoes. That seems to work well for them but I have discovered over the years (I initially hiked in tennis shoes) that I need the ankle support of a strong boot with sides!

7/2000

My boots are holding up well. I had an initial round of bad blisters but I tended them carefully & they healed - so now my feet feel fine! There are 4 women I've met who are hiking in bare feet - They say it's very comfortable!

(excerpt from letter)

What I Don't Carry

- **Shampoo:** My small container of camp suds will do for shampoo in a pinch, but usually I shampoo where there is a shower and there is some kind of shampoo there.

- **Deodorant:** I've given up using deodorant in both parts of my life; it doesn't seem necessary for me.

- **A wash cloth or towel:** I use my bandana as a wash cloth and a piece of clothing as a towel if I find I need one.

- **A Cell Phone:** For these reasons: it is added weight; there is seldom good reception; there is no way to charge it; many others do carry one and are willing to share if I desperately needed to make a call; but, most of all, it is such a disturbing feature in the middle of the beautiful, silent woods where life is simple!

What Have I Learned from My Hikes?

> One of the things I've learned out here is that anything is possible—whatever we need will somehow be supplied... Today Laurie, Maggie & I were standing in the middle of the woods by the GA/NC sign talking about having a picture taken—Maggie said, "We need another person to take it" and as we looked down the trail, along came a man who immediately took our picture!

Hiking is 99 percent mental and 1 percent anything else...

Dear Maria,

Re: What have you learned from hiking on the AT?

    I have learned so much about myself, my place in this world, what my needs are, etc . . . . Here is an abbreviated list, but know that there are many more things I could add to the list; periodically, a piece of Trail Wisdom pops into my head—something that I haven't written about. My sense is that I will continue to discover things that hiking has taught me—probably for the rest of my life.

    Well, the following is my list; I hope that by sharing it with you, you'll be encouraged to look at what you've learned from your own hiking and camping experiences. Know, also, that sometimes you will find that things about yourself that you already knew are totally reinforced when you test them out in the woods.

Love,
Aunt Peg

What I've Learned from Hiking on the AT

- I have reinforced the notion that I can do anything I put my mind to . . .
- I've learned that things always work out . . . to not worry so much about things . . . when you need something, it'll be there.
- I have learned that I am content with a simple life . . . the trappings/ details of a complicated life are not necessary for happiness or contentment or fulfillment.
- I have learned that I can ask others for help when I need it.
- I have learned that I need to take more time in my other life to just hang out.
- Also, I have learned that I don't need deodorant . . . I don't need to shave my legs . . . I don't need to shower every day . . . and, I can take a shower without a towel!

Day 49   Oct. 27, 2004
Cool, cloudy

Dear Susan + Tom,
    Greetings from the woods! We are in
North Carolina, high up in the mountains —
just 10 days to go to Springer Mtn., GA, the
end of the AT — It's hard to believe we
only have less than 150 miles to go —
    The hiking in the Smoky Mtns. was
fabulous — wonderful views, great trails — no
bear sightings, though! The shelters in that
section had wire cages around them that
we locked at night to keep the bears out!
    As before, there is so much more to this
experience than just hiking — we have loved
the network of trail people — other hikers,
friends who support hikers, townspeople, etc.
with my niece with me, we've been very
popular with everyone who is interested in
2 women hiking together.
    We have worked hard to reduce the
weight in our packs — initially we were
carrying 45–50 lbs. with full water + food — We
have gotten it down to 35 lbs. after a
re-supply!

– 2 –

People are always asking us questions like. "What have you learned out here?" "What's the most important thing you are carrying?" etc. … In response to what I've learned, perhaps. I'd say that you can always count on getting what you need — things always work out — also, it's OK to ask people for help — usually they are eager to help.

The most important "thing" I am carrying in my backpack (aside from water/ food) might be my sleeping bag liner — a new item this time that takes my 40° bag down to 25° or 30° + it weighs practically nothing (the liner, that is!).

This is all for now — — Take care.
♡ Peggy

Dear Nona + Fat,   7/2000

Many things about this hike are totally opposite of what they are in the olde life — for example, everyone is consumed with eating fat + calories. You have to because you burn so much — Also, being smelly + dirty is par for the course — The hiking shirts (that are the best (ie. they "wick" — breathe to keep you cool + they dry instantly) smell of perspiration all the time! It doesn't matter how much deodorant you use so I've given up deodorant! No one washes his/her hair more than once a week, if that. Mine was wet (from rain) for 4 straight days until I wore my ski hat to bed — it dried then but was quite a mess!
    More later — ♡ Peg

How Do I Plan a Hike/ Know Where to Go/Keep from Getting Lost?

White blazes on the trees mark the
Trail — That's how I know where to go —
I just follow the white marks! I
also have maps which give me details
along the way. 7/2000

Dear Maria,

You said you might be interested in a short hike on the AT . . . maybe the Maryland section. My friends Laurie, Brigid, and I have done just that so I thought I'd tell you how we planned it and then how it actually worked out.

 The MD section is only forty-two miles and many thru-hikers call it the tri-state challenge as they try to do it all in one day! From the south going north, they leave Harper's Ferry, West Virginia, do the forty-two miles in Maryland and end up in Pennsylvania . . . that means hiking into the night, but, I guess, that is doable for them; by that point in their thru-hikes, either Nobo* or Sobo*, they are well conditioned to do it. That's not, however, how we did it!

I always plan ahead using the trail maps, the Appalachian Trail Guide, and the Appalachian Thru-Hiker's Companion (all resources you can order online or get at REI* or other outfitter's stores). Information in those books help me know what the terrain looks like, where the shelters or campsites are, where the ascents and descents are, and where nearby towns are.

My plan for how far I go each day and where I stay at night is really dictated by the ascents and descents and resupply places. I can comfortably carry enough food for six to seven days but then I need to get supplies . . . Some hikers don't do that and instead just pack peanut butter, bagels, cheese, ramen noodles, and that's it! While I don't want to be anal about my food, it is important to me that I have a variety of healthy foods every day (probably because I think about food so much of the time!). The ascents and descents indicated on the trail maps also help me plan my days. I don't want to overload my day with too many high mountains to climb because that does slow me down; yet, if I see a stretch where it is pretty flat or a combination of climbing a mountain and then having a long descent, I know that will make for an easier hike and I can go further. I don't believe that the thru-hikers plan that way . . . they just seem to take each section as it is, but for those of us who are out for a defined period of time, this is all part of the planning so that you can start at one point and end up at another when you have to return to your other life!

So back to the Maryland trip . . . While I was planning, I came up with two scenarios for the amount of time we had for the hike. Both involved meeting Laurie and Brigid in Harper's Ferry, West Virginia, and leaving a car at the Park Headquarters in town. Uncle Marty then was to drive us to PenMar (the Pennsylvania-Maryland Park marking the state lines). While that looked like a bit of a distance (a little more than an hour), we had decided that we wanted to hike north to south, ending in Harper's Ferry.

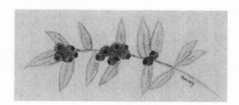

FYI: If you don't have a second car to drive you to a starting point or at the end point, there are many people who are willing to provide transportation. Anytime there is a hostel nearby, the people running the hostel often have a shuttle service. Don't be afraid to ask . . . if they can't do it, they'll usually know someone who can. I have become very bold about asking and have found people are more than willing to help. It might cost $10 or so, but it's worth it.

Potential Plans for the Maryland Hike

Plan #1

Monday: PenMar Park to Devil's Racecourse Shelter (five miles)
Tuesday: Devil's Racecourse Shelter to Covall Shelter (five miles)
Wednesday: Covall Shelter to PineKnob Shelter (eight miles)
Thursday: Pine Knob Shelter to Rocky Run Shelter (seven and a half miles miles)
Friday: Rocky Run Shelter to Ed Garvey Shelter (nine miles)
Saturday: Ed Garvey Shelter to WVA line (six miles)

Plan #2

Monday: PenMar to Devil's Racecourse Shelter (five miles)
Tuesday: Devil's Racecourse Shelter to Annapolis Rocks Campground (eleven miles)
Wednesday: Annapolis Rocks to Rocky Run Shelter (ten miles)
Thursday: Rocky Run to Ed Garvey Shelter (nine miles)
Friday: Ed Garvey Shelter to WVA line (six miles)

Maria,

Continuing on with the planning of the Maryland hike. After talking it over, we decided to do Plan #2 with the idea that if something went awry, we'd have an extra day to play with.

We then each planned and bought our own food for:

four breakfasts
five lunches
four dinners
snacks
and one emergency dinner
I'll include a list of the meals and snacks in a minute.

> FYI: I usually suggest that each person plan, carry, and cook his/her own food. That eliminates a whole process of decision making that can sometimes become complicated. That doesn't mean, though, that we don't sometimes share or cook meals together.

For this trip, I knew (because I had looked at the maps and guidebooks) that there was water at every campsite and shelter so that meant I didn't need to worry about carrying full water (which is very heavy). Also, hiking in the spring is different than in summer or fall when there has been a lot of dry weather . . . water is always available in spring!

I also knew from the guidebook that there would be hot showers at Dahlgren Campground (mile 23 from PenMar) which would be either day 3 or day 4, depending upon which plan we actually did—the anticipation of a hot shower is always motivating!

For such a short trip, there was no need to plan a resupply; however, if someone wanted to meet us or if we needed to get off the trail for some reason, there were several places in this section where that could happen. The guidebooks give specific directions to all those access areas, where to park, what to look for, etc.

> FYI: Always leave a copy of your itinerary with someone, as well as any information about access areas so you could be found if needed.

I'm going to include a day-to-day description of this hike to give you an idea of how a five-day hike for this section could easily be managed.

An Actual Hike: The Maryland Section

May 2009

Day 1: The three of us met in the morning at the Appalachian Trail Headquarters in Harper's Ferry, West Virginia. After lunch at a local café, Marty drove us north to the Pennsylvania-Maryland border. That took about an hour and a quarter with a bit of difficulty finding PenMar Park where the trailhead is located (the directions seem clear, but we had to stop to ask). Pen-Mar Park is a lovely large park and had bathroom facilities, as well as a source of water for filling our camelbacks.

At three o'clock we headed south on the trail for an easy five-mile hike; the guidebook does suggest that during this portion of the trail, we actually were at the highest point of the Maryland section of the trail. We arrived at Devil's Race Course Shelter a little after five. It was drizzling rain, so we set up our sleeping bags in the shelter and chatted with a thru-hiker who was already there.

Dinner for me was beef stew and a mini bagel; for dessert I had a cup of hot chocolate with a splash of brandy in it. I often find that my appetite is not huge the first couple of days I'm out, so often I have just one entree like I did this night.

Another hiker joined us and worked hard, with Laurie's help, to create a big bonfire. Later in the evening two sisters who were thru-hiking joined us; so the shelter was pretty full with five women, one man, and another man in his tent outside.

Day 2: We awoke to a beautiful day; the rain had stopped, the temperatures were in the sixties, and it promised to be a great hiking day. We tend to get up between six and seven, drink coffee or tea, have breakfast, get water, and then pack up. We are not usually in a hurry to make miles as some of the thru-hikers are. We still usually leave the campsite between eight thirty and nine in the morning. This morning was typical!

Breakfast for me was oatmeal and tea. Laurie and Brigid drink coffee using coffee bags; I do tea instead only because I like real cream in my coffee, and that's not available out in the woods.

So we set off around nine for an amazingly beautiful fourteen-mile day (not on the schedule plan, but it just happened!). The terrain was easy with no mountains to climb or major high/low points; the trail was rocky but not at all difficult to maneuver; our packs felt great (I was carrying about thirty-three pounds which is low for me). When we got to Annapolis Rocks where we had intended to camp, a group of teenagers from a school in New York City was there, so we pressed on to Pine Knob Shelter arriving about four.

Lunch for me was peanut butter and jam on a mini bagel.

Snacks during the morning included a hard-boiled egg and some gorp. In the afternoon, I ate part of a power bar and more gorp. And all the time I drink water, water, water!

Dinner was chicken and garlic mashed potatoes. For dessert I made hiker s'mores. Tea and brandy topped off the meal.

As we were relaxing at the shelter eating cheese and crackers before dinner, in came a hiker—a young man who was just stopping in for a break before pushing on four more miles. As it often happens, he proceeded to tell us his story . . .

He was seventeen years old, from Delaware where he had been homeschooled (the reason why he could be out hiking in mid-May) . . . he'd been on the trail for a little more than a week and was out for a month. His adventure had started one morning when he was awakened by his parents and told that the family was going out for breakfast. They got into the car and drove and drove (he said he figured something was up when they passed all the local breakfast places). At an AT crossing in Shenandoah National Park, they stopped the car, opened the trunk and there was a backpack—totally packed with all the equipment he'd need for a month. His parents told him to head North on the AT and they'd pick him up in New Jersey in a month!

As he told us this story, our mouths fell open and we said, "What did you do that was so bad?" Sheepishly, he admitted that he had not been easy to live with, had not followed his parents' rules and had been disrespectful to his mom . . . Moms ourselves, the three of us all said, "Why didn't we think of that?" As Drop-Off (his trail name) continued to talk, it was clear that he saw this opportunity as a good way to sort things out and to give his parents and himself a break from the tensions that adolescence creates for a family. He admitted that they were right in doing what they did and that he was secretly loving it. He commented that he knew things would be better when he returned home, and he was looking forward to starting over with his parents. Laurie took his picture and asked if it were OK with him to send it to his parents via e-mail. He was fine with that so once we got back from our hike, she sent the following e-mail:

Dear Nick's Mom and Dad,
I met your son, Nick, last week while hiking the Appalachian Trail in Maryland. I promised him that I would send you a photo and a note. First of all, let me say that he is a terrific young man and we were so happy to hear his story and to meet him. There were three of us "Moms" hiking together and it was refreshing to see a young man on the trail. He told us that you "surprised" him with the backpack and the hiking adventure because he was not behaving himself at home. The three of us agreed (after raising 7 children between us) that it was a BRILLIANT IDEA and wished we had thought of that with our own children!! Alas, it is too late. Our kids are grown. It seems the perfect age for instilling life's lessons without the day to day battles that only teenagers can create!

Have you hiked the AT before? I think so since Nick had everything he needed in his backpack. His trail name is "Drop Off".
Anyway, he seemed happy, comfortable, and remorseful for any trouble he has given to you. I think you will find him more mature when he returns home.

Good Luck and thanks for a great hiking story!

Laurie aka Sweetpatoty

It was an amazing story—but, then again, typical of the unique conversations we have with so many people on the trail.

So day 2 ended . . . I slept in my tent hammock for the first time which was very comfortable but a bit chilly . . . I need to put my sleeping mat underneath me in the hammock to block the cold coming up from the ground, just like I do when I am in my regular tent. Laurie and Brigid slept in the shelter; no other hikers joined us.

Day 3: This was a short, easy day. We hiked seven and a half miles over comfortable terrain, again no major ups or downs (this terrain is perfect for a first hike on the AT; some sections have at least one to two mountains to go up and over every day which can be challenging for a first-time hiker). Knowing that it would be a short day, we lounged at the shelter well past nine, having two cups of coffee/tea and our usual rounds of great conversation.

Breakfast for me was a bowl of oatmeal, a half bagel with peanut butter, jam, and tea.

Late in the morning we reached Washington Monument State Park which marks the beginning of an area with much historical significance. This park, in addition to the huge monument, is a park with all the amenities, i.e., running water, bathrooms, and road access. It is a great place for a day hike on the AT and is well used by families and others who want to get a taste of what the AT in Maryland is like.

Snacks this morning included another hard-boiled egg and some gorp, plus, of course, water!

From the park, it was a short distance on the trail to Old South Mountain Inn where we had hoped to have lunch—but, alas, it was closed for lunch. We decided to take a break in their parking lot anyway and sent Brigid to befriend the man mowing the lawn. Ultimately, he agreed to drive the ten minutes to a small town café and to bring back sandwiches for us and four other hikers who had congregated there with us. Getting real food on the trail is such a treat and we gratefully consumed tasty sub sandwiches for our lunch.

Back on the trail, we found Dahlgren campsites and showers not far from the Old South Mountain Inn. In another scenario, we could have pitched our tents at Dahlgren, had showers, and walked a short distance to the inn for a fancy gourmet dinner! Since our plans were otherwise, only Laurie showered while Brigid and I remained dirty and smelly and pushed on to Rocky Run Shelter. This shelter was in a lovely spot with a stream running in front and a separate dining platform off to the right of the shelter. We were early (three-ish) so settled in to relax and play some Farkle* before dinner. A thru-hiker, Gypsy, joined us around dinner time and turned out to be an amiable character. After hours of conversation about good books, teaching, life goals, along with some

Farkle, he pronounced that of all the nights he'd spent on the trail (seventy plus) that had been his most enjoyable!

Dinner for me was angel hair pasta with pesto—one of my favorites. Pieces of chocolate, hot tea, and brandy were dessert.

We all slept in the shelter together as the trees did not position themselves for convenience in setting up my tent hammock—the only drawback to having that as my alternative to shelter lodging.

Day 4: This was another great day—weather and terrain were perfect for hiking. We had nine miles to go to meet Sarah (Brigid's daughter) at the Ed Garvey Shelter where we were all spending the night.

Breakfast for me was oatmeal once again!

We arrived in Gathland State Park about noon. With time to spare, we enjoyed reading all the signs about the history of the area relating to the Civil War. The arch monument to the memory of the Civil War news correspondents was prominent in that park. We also enjoyed the presence of real bathrooms, a water pump, a garbage can, as well as a long leisurely lunch break.

Lunch for me was tuna fish mixed with mayo on a bagel which I love! Snacks were the usual: gorp.

From there, we scurried along the trail, hoping to reach the Ed Garvey Shelter before Sarah and the dogs (her dog Bonnie and Brigid's cutest dog in the world Little Eddie) arrived. As it turned out, we did the nine miles in four hours so arrived at Ed Garvey in midafternoon. The Ed Garvey is the premier shelter among Maryland shelters. Recently built, it features an upstairs and downstairs. Plexiglas encloses the upstairs area which is reached by a set of stairs in the back of the shelter; the first floor is typical three-sided/open in front platform but larger than most of the shelters we stay in. This one with both levels probably sleeps twenty hikers easily and more than that on a cold rainy night. A picnic table, fire pit, and logs for sitting make the area very inviting for groups of hikers. The privy is one of the best on this section of the trail; however, this time it was closed for renovations so we had to use the area below the privy for bathroom use.

This shelter is about a three-mile hike from a parking area and makes a great day hike or hike to see if backpacking and staying in a shelter is to your liking! I often take people who want to hike on the AT with me to this section for a day hike.

Sarah arrived with the dogs about an hour after we did; she had parked on the road and hiked the three miles in. She brought subs for dinner for all of us which we immediately ate. We built a fire and entertained her with our stories from the trail. For dessert, I made a fruit cobbler for us all to share; hot chocolate and tea ended the evening.

No one else joined us at the shelter so we faced the dilemma of whether to sleep upstairs or downstairs. We settled on downstairs because it was easier for the dogs. This was the first camping experience for both Bonnie and Little Eddie and they spent much of the night snuggled among the sleeping bags. Bonnie was clueless as to what was happening, but Little (Perfect) Eddie was scared out of his mind and worried that we had gone to sleep and were not guarding him. They did not sleep well!

Day 5: We arose early, prepared, and ate our usual breakfasts: Mine was oatmeal and tea! The lure of town food was strong, so I did not have the usual big appetite. We left about nine and hiked the six miles into Harper's Ferry, having completed the total forty-two miles in the Maryland section. The hike from Ed Garvey to town is delightful as it follows switchbacks down about 2.5 miles, crosses a road, and follows the C&O Canal Towpath for a couple of miles straight into town where there are many restaurants, cafes, etc. We found one where we could sit outside with the dogs and eat great hamburgers. When I hike, I crave hamburgers . . . juicy and full of fat! So this was perfect, especially when we topped it off with ice cream.

We had left Laurie's car in a parking lot at the Park Center, so she and I caught a bus to take us the ten minutes to the lot. We picked up her car and returned to the restaurant for Brigid, Sarah, and the dogs.

As always, it is bittersweet to say goodbye to our hiking world and return to our other lives; yet, the magic of the woods stays inside us and before we know it we are planning our next trip!

Details to Think about as You Plan a Hike . . .

- How should you get physically ready for a hike?

Before my first two-month hike in 2000, I started in January to wear my hiking boots everywhere to break them in. I also walked almost every day, sometimes two miles, sometimes five or six miles, and I wore my backpack (partially full). The week before I started the hike in June, I totally filled my backpack and walked with it . . . and pulled a muscle (it precipitated two to three emergency trips to the chiropractor). I was only somewhat ready!

Before the two-month hike in 2004, I swam, kayaked, and hiked all summer with regularity—my normal summer in Maine activities anyway. I discovered the concept of muscle memory that summer and realized that the reason it wasn't hard to get back into hiking on the AT was that my body muscles remembered . . . "this is what we have to do!" I had felt initially in 2000 that my muscles rebelled for about two weeks and then finally realized that hiking was what they had to get used to. So now before any other hike, I start at least two to three weeks ahead of time with the walking/boots/backpack and go out every day. In Maryland, our driveway is a steep hill, so I use that as a gauge for when I'm ready—if I can hike up that hill easily, I'm ready. In Maine, I have a variety of hikes I do ahead of time.

I believe, though, that every hiker has his/her own way of getting ready physically. Laurie plays tennis and crews; Brigid runs and works out at the gym . . . so my advice is to build in some physical exercise that works for you.

For long-distance or thru-hikers, the saying on the trail is that the first two weeks of hiking are what get you into shape—so go slow at first and get your body acclimated to the day-to-day work on the trail.

- How much money should you take with you, and what do you spend it on?

I usually take $20-$30 in cash and try to have a few $1 bills in the mix. Then I have a credit card as well. I keep my money, my card, and my license (for identification) in a small Ziploc bag in the pouch around my waist.

Depending upon how long you are out hiking, there are many ways to spend money on the trail (yes, in the woods!). If you pass by a store, you'll need money for the donut or ice cream or whatever you think you must have! If you decide unexpectedly to spend the night at a hostel or motel, you'll need money. If you need a shuttle to/from the trailhead, you'll need money. For a long-distance or thru-hike, you may need money to replace/repair equipment, to resupply, etc.

When I am in Maine, I also carry a blank check from my Maine checking account. That came in handy the year we hired the seaplane to transport us ahead on the trail!

- What do you do about garbage on the trail?

The policy all along the AT is carry in/carry out so be prepared to carry your garbage unless it is paper (not plastic) that you can burn in a fire pit. I use my used Ziploc bags for garbage and keep them in the very top of my backpack on the chance that I'll pass by a garbage can or find someone who offers to take my garbage (sometimes day hikers will do that).

In the Maryland section, we were pleased to find garbage cans in the Gathland State Park and Washington Monument State Park as well as the parking lot at Old South Mountain Inn. Whenever the trail passes through a town, obviously you can get rid of your garbage; also, you can get water that doesn't have to be treated—which is a real treat.

WHAT IS IT LIKE TO FINISH A LONG-DISTANCE HIKE AND GO BACK TO THE OTHER LIFE?

8/12/2000

Dear Marcella,
I climbed Mt. Katahdin yesterday to mark the end of my hike. In June I had seen a sign in Mass. that said "Mt. Katahdin - 681 miles." It was amazing to remember that as I stood on top of the mountain. I've lost 10-12 lbs.—all my body fat is gone!! I'm enjoying putting back the weight!
I hope you are loving London.
See you soon. ♡ Peggy

July 31, 2000

... this trip has been all I had hoped it would be. I have tackled many mountains, including the White Mtns. & Mt. Washington. I've hiked in the rain, in the heat, in the mud & in the cold!

The other night Maggie, Niko, and I decided on the spur of the moment to camp out on top of a mountain instead of going to the shelter— we watched the most beautiful sunset and then an even more beautiful sunrise. I will miss having opportunities to do that when I get back to my other life.   11/2004

We can never go back . . . we will never be the same as we were before we started the hike . . .

—Goose Downs

Dear Maria,

I guess I should tell you what it's like for me when I finish a hike and return to my other life! Actually, I imagine you might identify with some of what I'm going to tell you because whether you've been in the hiking world for two months or two weeks or two days, the exit from that life is probably similar—bittersweet, I think, is the word to describe the feelings.

On the one hand, I always feel such a sense of accomplishment. In my circle of friends, I'm the only one I know who has hiked 700 miles in two months; it does set me apart from others and not in a bad way. The accomplishment, besides hiking the miles, is also the completion of a goal I set out to do—I said I was going to hike from Connecticut to Maine, and I did . . . and I not only survived, but thrived with a ton of incredible memories. I tested my body, my will, and my resolve which is always good to do (I think!) at different times in your life . . . Also, there is no doubt that I am happy to get back to the company of Uncle Marty and the comfortable routine we have together in our lives . . . as well as the amenities of home, e.g., water from the faucet, daily showers, toilets that flush, etc.

On the other hand, I really miss the hiking life and find myself frequently thinking of images from the trail . . . views of the woods as you wake up in the shelters, ridge walks, hard rain on the shelter roof, being on top of a mountain watching a sunset, tall pines in the mist (looking like scenes from *Braveheart*!) and on and on . . .

Initially when I get off the trail, I feel overwhelmed when I'm in places with a lot of people, particularly in stores . . . it's so different from being in the woods by yourself. I also find that the details of the other life tend to irritate me, e.g., the dishwasher doesn't work, there is laundry for many people to be done, etc. It always takes me a while to settle back into that life.

I find that people's reactions to and questions about the hike are hard to handle. Actually, what I have figured out is that people probably don't know what to say or ask because they don't have a frame of reference—so they tend to ask generic questions, "So how was your hike?"—a very hard question to answer briefly! I have practiced my answer to that as I get it so frequently and am not content to just say, "Great!" Often these days, I say something along the lines of, "It was an amazing dip into a very different life and I loved it." Really astute friends might then respond, "So what adventures did you have?" or "Are you finding it hard to come back to this life?" You, Maria, had the perfect comment to me once when you said, "Sometimes you just have to get outside by yourself"—short, to the point, it gave me the sense that you completely understood.

The hardest part, I think, of coming back to the other life is how to hang on to the feelings I have in my day-to-day hiking life—being outside, living simply, not being caught up in complicated situations, and knowing things will always work out. When I can't be in the woods hiking, I still want to have a sense about me of the simple contentment, being in the moment, and clearheadedness that I get from my hiking life.

So in response to the question "What's it like to get back to your other life after a hike?" my answer is "Not easy!" But I do work every day at focusing on what I need to do to live simply and contentedly in the midst of a sometimes chaotic world.

Well, Maria, I've rambled on long enough . . . I've told all I can think of about the AT and the wonderful adventures I've had, as well as the life I've lived on it! I hope you will continue to be inspired to hike, camp, and live your life the way you want . . . you seem to be well on your way to doing that. Please know that I am there cheering you on, supporting your choices, and knowing that all will work out for you.

Love,
Aunt Peg

Maria,

On my really long hikes (two months), I usually lose weight—particularly a lot of my body fat. I return to the other life with an incredible appetite that just doesn't go away because I've stopped hiking! In mid-August 2000, I stopped hiking; I had lost twelve pounds, and while I ate huge quantities of food, I never felt full until near Christmas! It took me about a year to gain back the twelve pounds . . .

Once when I had been hiking for several weeks, I walked into a shelter to the smell of someone smoking a cigar—suddenly, I had huge homesick pangs for Uncle Marty! I do miss him greatly when I am away . . .

Maria,

In 2000 when I came back from my hike, I felt extremely clearheaded—as if all the extra, unimportant stuff in my head was cleared out. What an incredible feeling!

11/7/04

Dear Suz,

Well... we finished on Thursday on top of Springer Mountain — It poured rain almost the whole day, but cleared as we did the final stretch — Springer is very low key compared to the other end — Mt. Katahdin in Maine — but it was great to get there, sit on the rocks in the woods, take the pictures, feel the sense of accomplishment...

We stayed in the shelter on top & had the coldest night of the whole trip! Luckily, there were 5 of us there so some body heat was generated. Friday we hiked the 8.8 miles to the state Park (it's called the Approach Trail) — then went into the lodge to eat lunch — while we were there, a couple — Brenda + Regie Price (the Carolina Creepers) whom I'd met in 2000 when I hiked & have been in touch with — came in to surprise us!! They drove 5 hours from their home in South Carolina to meet us at the end. We had a wonderful visit & ended up leaving the park to stay at a motel in Dahlonega about 10 miles away — They spent the night

-2-

there too + we had a chance to catch up on everything. They are in their 60's— Finished the trail in 2001 + the next year biked from coast to coast → CA to Florida! Remarkable people in every way—

So now, we are still in the Econo Lodge, waiting for Mark + Shelley to pick us up so we can head home to Maryland. It's been an incredible trip—hiking with Maggie has been such fun—we've not really been concerned about the "schedule," yet ended up when we thought we would—we've been very flexible + have done many more things than I'd have done if I'd been alone. Again, like before we have many new friends—Hiking + staying together in shelters day after day creates great bonds with people, very quickly. Probably one of the greatest parts of this hike has been the people we've met.

It'll be hard to get back to the "other" world—I'll let you know about that when I write next week! ♡ Peg

Dear Suz,   10/31/04

— The last Sunday on the trail — it's Halloween night so we've been celebrating with a great campfire, an "exchange" of candy treats from our food bags and scarey stories around the campfire. My friend Laurie is here with us, along with Niko from NY + Zero from Texas.

It's been a really fun week with Laurie + now we only have 71 miles left. We crossed into Georgia today so the time is quickly slipping away. Mark, Shelley + the boys will pick us up on Sunday AM + drive us back to Maryland.

Life out here is simple — which is wonderful! I needed to be away from stress for a while + this has been perfect... it's a dip into a whole other life/culture — one where people of all ages are equal + the talk is about nature, the hike, and philosophical issues rather than day to day problems. It'll be hard to leave, but I'll be glad to see Marty + Jeff again.

It'll be good to get back to my own cooking + regular food! I've probably lost 8-10 lbs. + have a huge appetite — Right now I'm craving apple pie!

Talk to you soon —
                                Love, Peg

Journal Entry - 11/28/04

...I have to confess that I'm really kidding myself when I tell people that I am adjusting well to being back after hiking for two months. It has not been easy and I find myself longing for that other world which was so simple, "in the moment," and lacking stress. I miss being outside terribly and I feel plagued by the unpleasant details of this life...

RAINY

...Yesterday I was driving on Rt. 70 to Frederick - I found myself looking at the mountains in the distance + wondering, "How many miles from here to the top of that mountain by foot!

Dear Maria,

Re: What was your favorite section of the trail?

Now, that's a hard question to answer because I loved it all! The most challenging sections were in the north, i.e., New Hampshire and Maine, each having its own flavor. Getting into Maine felt like coming home, and the closer I got to Mt. Katahdin, the more the excitement built up. The trail in Maine is varied with a lot of roots and rocks, mountains that were rugged, fir trees, pine sidewalks, etc. The Mahoosuc Notch in Southern Maine was by far the hardest section of the whole trail and continues to be the barometer from which I measure all hard challenges in my life . . . "If I could do Mahoosuc Notch, then I can do anything" is my mantra. I believe that the beauty of the Maine woods is imprinted on me from childhood, so once I passed the New Hampshire border into Maine in the middle of the woods, I felt the comfort of places I knew and things that were familiar to me . . . so for those reasons, I often say Maine was my favorite part, particularly, also, because my all-time favorite mountain is at the end of that section.

However, in the fall of 2004, when I did the long-distance hike from Daleville, Virginia, to Springer Mountain, Georgia, I found that hiking through the Smoky Mountains in Tennessee and North Carolina in October was a spectacular experience. As I think about it, it seems to me that my favorite sections may have more to do with the people I was with or met than the actual terrain. All sections are beautiful in their own way so other influences, e.g., people, weather, bugs, etc., tend to create the positive or negative feelings I would have for a section . . . so there you have it, Maria!

♡ aunt Peg

Excerpts from my journal

...as I go about the business of living in this world, I carry inside my head a whole fantasy world — one filled with thoughts of a simple life spent walking through the woods, loving the beauty of shades of green, climbing high mountains to the top, scrambling over rocks, sleeping snugly in my tent, listening to the sounds of animals around me....It is a "world" that I don't always share out loud, but it is what gets me through the challenges of the high-tech, fast-paced, expectation-driven society of which I am also a part...

RAINY

...when I walked to the mailbox this morning I heard the call of the bird I always hear mornings on the trail, particularly when I first come out of my tent.... perhaps he is calling me to the trail —

...as I stepped out of the house on this cold, crisp February morning, I suddenly thought:
"AT hikers are starting in Georgia today."
I had a wistful thought — It could be me!

Dear Maria,

In May 2010, I finally finished all of the AT. I had done everything except for New York and New Jersey (162 miles), so I hiked for thirteen days in late April to early May to complete the entire trail. Thought you might like to read my journal entry from May 17, 2010, which pretty much sums up what I have to say about the whole hike.

I have finished the AT. I have hiked 2,176 miles in ten years. I have walked the trail in all the states, following the white blazes. While I started in 1997 when I was fifty, I actually tell people that my starting point was in 2000 which was my first two-month hike—making it an even ten years.

At the beginning, I don't think I realized the magnitude of walking the trail. It seemed like just something I wanted to do—a lark, perhaps. It wasn't until I was actually on the trail that I realized how life changing and addictive hiking would become. It has been a ten-year process of discovery for me—who I am, what my life could be like, what my vision is for living life . . . similar to a ten-year "vision quest."

I started the hike in a very busy time of my life—I was still working many jobs and trying to capture a few moments here and there to be outside . . . over the ten years I have retired twice, worked many jobs, worked no jobs, seen a good friend die of cancer, seen my mother die, written and published a book on women's wisdom, started writing a journal, and decided I'm a minimalist . . . and here I am ten years later: sixty-three years old—still energized and active—moving ahead at a pace that is comfortable and allows for reflection, being in the moment . . . living the life I want to live. Hiking the whole AT is an accomplishment, a goal, but it's more than that—it's a transformation or perhaps the transition to a fuller life, one where I know who I am, how I want to live—one where life is replete with peaceful moments, contentment, and fulfillment . . . I do the things I want to do . . . I know what I want to do, I am confident, happy, and reflective . . . I enjoy my own company, as well as the company of others . . . Time on the trail has allowed me to grow into this life, these feelings, shaping the vision of how life should be for me.

May 17, 2010

Dear Maria,

It occurred to me that throughout the letters in this book, I have often used terms or made reference to jargon that is specific to the AT. While the language of the trail is commonplace to me, it may not always be familiar to you or other readers, so . . . I'm going to include a list of vocabulary and definitions, sort of a glossary of terms that might be helpful to you—I know, once a teacher, always a teacher!

Love,
Aunt Peg

Blueberry's AT Vocabulary Glossary of Terms

- Bear bell: A small bell attached to the backpack; as you hike, it makes a jingling sound which alerts bears and other animals that you are on the trail. Bears do not like to be surprised, so this is a polite way of letting them know you are there! Mine is an antique sheep's bell—small with a lovely sound.

- Bear poles: Some areas on the AT, i.e., the section in the Shenandoahs and the section in the Smokies, have these poles. They are for storing your food at night so the bears or other animals don't get it. They differ in design, depending upon the site, but do consist of tall poles with a pulley system to hoist and lower the food bags.

- Breakfast cookies: One of my staples, these cookies can be eaten anytime for quick energy. Recipe can be found on page 106.

- Dime sighting: This is a term unique to me and my family but can best be described as finding dimes in very unusual places. In our family, we believe that the dimes are placed in these places by our dad, who died in 1997, as a sign that he is still watching over us. Twice on the AT trip in 2004, Maggie and I found dimes, once under a picnic table and once on the floor of a shelter. We describe the finding of these dimes as dime sightings.

- Farkle: A dice game I carry in my backpack; we play this often at night with other hikers on the floors of the shelters. It is easy to learn, very light to carry, and can be played by people of all ages. Directions for this game are on page 165.

- GA—ME or ME—GA: The sign used by hikers to indicate that they are hiking from Georgia to Maine or Maine to Georgia.

- Flipflop: This is a term used to describe a hike that is started in one direction and then the hiker gets a ride to the other end and finishes the hike by hiking to where he left off. This is often used when a hiker starts in the south, heads north, and realizes he/she won't be able to be at the end in the north before snow/bad weather comes; by stopping at some point around the middle and being transported to the northern end, the hiker is able to finish the whole hike in one season.

- Hiker hostel: In the towns along the trail there are many of these hostels. They cater to AT hikers and vary in their amenities. Usually they provide beds, a bathroom, and showers; often they include a place to do laundry, kitchen facilities, and shuttle services. They are very inexpensive and provide a charming, although often rustic, respite for long-distance or thru-hikers who have been sleeping outdoors for many days.

- Hiking bars: A recipe from my friends, Laurie and Brigid, these bars are delicious and can be used for breakfast, lunch, dinner, and/or snacks; they are packed with powerful energy! Recipe can be found on page 106.

- 100-mile wilderness: Starting in Monson, Maine, this is the last stretch of the AT before reaching Mt. Katahdin in Baxter State Park. For many years once a hiker started the trek through the 100-mile wilderness, there was no access in or out until Baxter Park. These days there are a number of logging roads which have access to the trail, and there is the White House landing, a fishing lodge/hiker hostel on a lake, which can be reached by a side trail and a boat ride.

- Huts: On the AT, the huts are a system of lodges in the White Mountains. About seven miles apart/a day's hike, these are buildings with bunk rooms (dormitory style), a gathering room, bathrooms (no showers), and breakfast and dinner prepared and served by college students. The food, accommodations, and camaraderie at the huts make these a welcome stop for long-distance hikers, as well as weekend hikers. See article, "Friendship on the Trail," on page 56.

- Nobo: Northbound on the trail, i.e., Nobo hiker.

- Sobo: Southbound on the trail, i.e., Sobo hiker.

- REI (Recreational Equipment Inc.): This is an outfitter store chain where I buy most of my equipment. There are many other outfitter stores along the length of the trail which are similarly able to provide quality equipment and service to hikers.

- Resupply: This process for getting more food/supplies while hiking is usually accomplished in towns/stores near the trail or mail drops at post offices along the trail. Hikers usually resupply every six to eight days.

- Ridge runner: A person employed by the AT association to hike a certain section of the trail and assist hikers in distress or to note unusual activity on the trail.

- Shelter book/journal: In each shelter there is a journal. Hikers usually sign in and often write a message. Sometimes the message is to other hikers; sometimes it is about part of the hike. Entries in the journals/ books could be used to find a hiker or to check on where a hiker is headed, in case of an emergency from the outside world. Typically, the hikers use their trail names when they sign the book. See Trail Names, page 65.

- Shelter/lean-to: All along the AT, every eight to twelve miles, are three-sided structures called shelters. They are usually located near a water source and have a privy. Ranging in size, some accommodate six to eight hikers, others twelve to fifteen. Some have picnic tables and fire rings. AT guidebooks and maps indicate where the shelters are located, and many hikers use the shelter destinations as a way of planning their hikes.

- Slack-packing: This is a term used to describe the situation where a hiker leaves his/her big pack at a hostel or in town, hikes for a day without the burden of a heavy pack, and then is picked up by someone to be transported back to a place to stay for the night.

- Thru-hikers: Hikers who are completing the whole Appalachian Trail in one time period, i.e., five to six months.

- Trail magic: This is like a random act of kindness! It is usually in the form of a surprise package of food somewhere along the trail, e.g., a box of snacks, cold sodas in a cooler of ice or in a stream, homemade cookies in a bag hanging from a tree branch, a candy bar left on top of your backpack, etc. The givers are usually anonymous and are often referred to as trail gnomes or trail angels. Trail magic can also be the appearance, seemingly out of the blue, of something or someone you really need, e.g., a person who appeared to take our picture in the woods of Georgia (see letter on page 194).

- Trail names: These are names hikers use instead of their own names. It helps preserve their anonymity and is an easy way for other hikers to remember them. My trail name is Blueberry. (See letter on page 65.)

- White blaze: These blazes, painted on trees all along the trail, mark the whole route from Georgia to Maine. These blazes are designed to keep hikers from getting off trail or lost.

- Yellow blazing: Getting a ride in a car to skirt part of the AT, this is used to move ahead on the trail. Once Laurie, Brigid, and I got a ride in a seaplane to move ahead twenty miles—we wondered if the term for that was sky blazing!

- Zero day: A day of no hiking—typically a day in town or at a hostel to rest and/or resupply.

Dear Maria,

You are probably thinking, "Who are all these people Aunt Peg wrote letters to while she was hiking!" I know you recognize some of the names, i.e., Uncle Marty (for sure!), my sister Mary, my mom, my sister Martha and husband Dave, your cousins VJ and Tony, Nanny, and the rest of the Stouts . . . The others are all friends of mine who were interested in my hikes. Some are hikers; others are armchair hikers. There are several letters to Suz . . . she and I have been friends for forty-plus years, and we write letters to each other every Sunday (have been doing that for fifteen years), so on the trail, whenever it was Sunday, I wrote to her; she faithfully kept them all and returned them to me when I got home.

Overall, I probably wrote and sent more than two hundred letters during the ten years it took me to complete the whole AT. I really was overwhelmed by all who responded to me, saving and returning the letters. At least 75 percent of the letters were returned to me, so I had many to choose from when I began to compile the letters for this book.

When I was selecting which letters to include, I found that often I'd written letters with similar content to more than one person, so sometimes letters are not included because a similar one was. I do hope that my family and friends understand that!

♡ aunt Peg

ACKNOWLEDGMENTS

To my family and friends:

The ten-year journey which began on the Appalachian Trail has culminated in this book. As the by-product of the accomplishments of a fifty-plus-year-old woman, it reflects and encapsulates the notion that one woman's goal was achieved through the support, encouragement, advice, and reason from friends and family throughout the journey.

All of you know who you are: some of you have been my hiking partners well before I announced that I was going to hike the AT, some of you I hiked with on the AT, some of you I met as new friends while I was hiking the AT, some of you shuttled me and brought me resupply packages, some of you have listened to me talk about my hiking for hours, some of you were willing to question my sanity, but still encouraged me . . .

But . . . all of you inspired me with your messages, questions, and enthusiasm about what I was doing . . .

So I acknowledge my gratitude to each of you for your presence in my regular life, as well as my hiking life . . .

Additionally, I must express my love and gratitude to my husband, Marty, who was my constant cheerleader, the one who always believed in my dream but who was also the voice of reason. From hiking with me in our early days, to driving to and from trailheads, to sending packages, to maintaining life on the home front, to graciously handling the questions of "How can you let her do this?", and to editing this book, he has been the solid force behind my hikes.